HITLER'S LIES

An Answer to Hitler's *Mein Kampf*

HITLER'S LIES

An Answer to Hitler's *Mein Kampf*

BANNED IN NAZI GERMANY

IRENE HARAND

JAICO PUBLISHING HOUSE

Ahmedabad Bangalore Chennai
Delhi Hyderabad Kolkata Mumbai

Published by Jaico Publishing House
A-2 Jash Chambers, 7-A Sir Phirozshah Mehta Road
Fort, Mumbai - 400 001
jaicopub@jaicobooks.com
www.jaicobooks.com

HITLER'S LIES:
AN ANSWER TO HITLER'S MEIN KAMPF
ISBN 978-81-8495-070-0

Originally published as
His Struggle – The Answer to Hitler from Irene Harand

First Jaico Impression: 2010
Fifth Jaico Impression: 2021

Printed by
Trinity Academy For Corporate Training Limited, Mumbai

Contents

Foreword

The following book by Madame Irene Harand seems to me to be a triumphant answer to the fallacious arguments, arrogant assumptions and unwarranted actions of the German dictator, Adolf Hitler. In her preface, Madame Harand claims to have written a book for the people, and in my opinion underestimates the real scholarship of her work. She says, "I do not turn to scholars," but I think that even scholars can learn much from this valuable work.

Perhaps the saddest pages of history are those that describe religious and racial persecution. Twenty years ago there were many who thought that such things could never again happen in this world, but the recent sad history of some of the countries of Europe proves how little foundation such hopes had.

Madame Harand has directed her attack against Hitler's persecution of the Jews on the sound ground that Anti-Semitism debases Christianity. She has successfully exploded the myth of racial and national superiority. No one who reads this book will again be inclined to assert the fallacy of Nordic superiority. Madame Harand has also dealt triumphantly with the lies about the Jews, and the list of the distinguished Jews in all lines of human endeavor which she gives from page 180 to 216 will be useful to any scholar. This list also should prove even to Hitler the tremendous loss he is imposing upon Germany, not to say upon the rest of the world, when he attempts to bar distinguished Jewish professors from the universities and distinguished doctors and lawyers from their respective professions.

Apart from all other considerations, persecution of races and religion has always failed. If persecution ever succeeded the Jews would long since have vanished from the earth and the history of Christianity proves beyond all doubt the futility of persecution. Cardinal Faulhaber has stated the matter well in a quotation which Madame Harand uses in this book, when he says,

"The Jews are persecuted all over the world but the methods of persecution in our country are a shame and a disgrace to us. History has taught that God always punishes the tormentors of the Jewish people. . . . The Jews will not be exterminated by hatred and persecution. The oldest people in the world has already gone through much suffering. They suffer now and will always suffer because they have remained true to their great faith. We must honor and esteem them for they have given the world the most glorious and invaluable gift—the Bible. Enlighten your brothers, tell them that racial hatred is a wild and poisonous growth in our life. Eradicate from your hearts this dreadful and inhuman prejudice against the eternal suffering people."

Madame Harand, in writing this book has done a distinguished service to Christianity and humanity. This English translation will serve to enlighten all readers of the English language on what is really going on in Germany.

J. W. R. Maguire, C.S.V
June 5, 1937-

Preface

After Hitler s seizure of power in Germany, I directed a few enlightening words to my fellow Christians in the form of a brochure to prove to them that anti-Semitism debases Christianity. Since then more than two years have glided by. Much blood has been spilled in Germany, and many tears have been shed there.

The ruthless force of the Nazis has been directed against the Jewish and Catholic minorities. Their main attack, however, has been launched against German Jewry, which has had to bear unspeakable torture and humiliation in the Third Reich. They foster and unleash hatred against the Jews and commit wholesale murder to maintain a power they have wrested from others. It, therefore, lies in the interest of truth to make public answer to the Nazi bible, "My Struggle," and to ascertain whether the main doctrines of this book, upon which the Nazi political state is founded, can bear critical examination before the civilized world.

This analysis of the Nazis has been sorely needed to expose their horrible assault on Christianity and Jewry which violates those primary rights of man respected as a matter of course in every civilised country. It is the duty of the entire civilised world to protest vigorously the brutalities to which Jews and Christians have been subjected in Germany.

The Nazis do not stop at defaming and harassing German Jews, German Catholics and other Christians who still remain true to their Savior. It is their desire to expand their rule over the entire universe and to incite all peoples to follow the bloody example they have set. For this reason I wish to point out the dangers to humanity inherent in any increased momentum of the Swastika forces. Perhaps I will succeed in exposing these factors to the eyes of those in Germany who have not lost every feeling of shame. Perhaps the high army leaders in Germany will realize what noble service they would render their fatherland were they to throw the Nazis out of office.

I have treated the racial question in general and the Jewish question in particular. I have questioned whether the racial question should be granted the importance that the Nazis ascribe to it. Were the racial ideology to collapse, the Nazis would lose one of their most important weapons. I have also questioned whether the Jews possess such physical and spiritual defects as to justify the bloody Nazi crusade against them. I believe I have proved that the "hereditary substance" of the modern Jews is definitely not of inferior calibre. If we seek an evaluation of the Jews of today under the microscope of history and science, we are confronted with findings quite different from those of the Nazis. By citing several episodes from Jewish history, quoting important doctrines from the

Talmud and calling special attention to the cultural accomplishments of contemporary Jews, I have illustrated how the treatment of the Jews in Germany amounts to nothing more than brutal intimidation and cowardly persecution of a defenseless minority by an overwhelming majority. The opponents of Hitler, unfortunately, have written very little about the Jewish question. A great deal more should be said of the persecution mania of the Nazis. They should be deprived of any pseudo-moral justification for their atrocities. I have pointed out the mendacity of the accusations leveled against our Catholic faith, depicted other conditions in Germany and described the Nazi attack on Austria. To substantiate my attitude I have cited the opinions of numerous ecclesiastical and mundane authorities.

I do not turn to scholars! I want to be understood by the people. Consequently my language and style may not please all bel esprits.

The object of this book is to convince the Christian peoples of the falsity of the Nazi doctrines and to warn them against the frightful menace of German National Socialism. I hope that it will bring consolation to the victims of National Socialism. It ought to assure them that there are still some people in this world who will not submit to the terror of the Third Reich but who will fight until the danger of Nazi expansion is banished from the earth and the victims of National Socialism are rescued from their torturers.

Irene Harand.

***Vienna, June* 193 5.**

CHAPTER I

Lies, the Main Weapon of the Nazis

The most effective and most formidable weapon of the Nazis is their propaganda. In "Mein Kampf," page 200, Hitler writes:

"The task of propaganda is not to weigh the rights of each side, but to emphasize exclusively the one thing that is to take the place of the other through the medium of propaganda. Propaganda does not have to state the truth objectively, insofar as it is favorable to the others, nor to place the truth before the masses in doctrinary candor, but must serve its own interests uninterruptedly. It was basically wrong to discuss the war guilt from the point of view that Germany alone could not be made responsible for the outbreak of this catastrophe. The right way would have been to place the entire blame on the enemy, even if this did not really correspond to the true course of events, as actually was the case."

This passage indicates Hitler's approval of lies and calumnies as weapons of destruction. Nothing else matters but the goal. To attain this, the Nazis teach, the way may lead through falsifications and distortions.

The Swastika concepts that the truth must not be imparted to the people, lest it make them dangerous, and that personal rights must not be considered, are false doctrines.

The Nazis have planted a virulent poison in the souls of youth. God bequeathed speech unto people so that they could understand one another. Whoever lies to his neighbor has abused this gift.

The lie is a filthy weapon, the lie is a crime against God, against Nature and against Humanity. That is why I wish to expose the Nazis. The world must know that the Nazi victory was won through contempt for religion, ethics and morals, and through the violation of truth and justice. It is the duty of all peoples and all nations to unite against National Socialism, to isolate this plague within the borders of the Third Reich and to liberate the millions of unfortunates who still languish in the German animal cage.

CHAPTER 2

Rabid Nationalism

The Nazis consciously foster arrogance and false pride. The Germans are told that they are superior to other people and that every German should be proud to belong to this chosen race. Hitler envies the French because they "were not educated in objectivity" but "in the most subjective manner conceivable."

A state is a member of the family of nations that constitutes the world. No nation can afford to be burdened with a hatred of, or a feeling of superiority toward, another nation. Nationalism, when implanted in youth, acts as a poison, stirring up from within, hatred of all other branches of humanity. Such nationalism leads to war.

I consider myself a good Austrian. I am greatly devoted to my Fatherland. It was essentially love for my country that impelled me to fight against Austria's becoming a Nazi province. I began my battle publicly long before Hitler's seizure of power; I frankly expressed my attitude in meetings at a time when it was not known how the battle would end.

I loved my people too much to see them ground under the heel of the Nazi terror. My patriotism must not be confused with nationalism.

National arrogance is the brainchild of politicians and opportunists. Knowing of no other way to delude the masses without rendering them real aid, they resort to rabid nationalism, which costs them nothing and which serves their purpose beautifully by awakening and nurturing egoistic instincts. If our forefathers had performed heroic deeds or had distinguished themselves in the sciences or in the arts, we would have the satisfaction of perpetuating a renowned name and of knowing that our stock had contributed to human progress. A chauvinist, however, would use this geneology to bolster up his own arrogance. It is an outrage to balance the fate of humanity on so uncertain a basis as chauvinism. It is not my intention in the slightest to minimize the accomplishments of the German nation. What I object to is that any nation should designate itself as a chosen people. Do the Nazis contend that the French have no right to extol the greatness of their fatherland and to "feel a justified pride in belonging to a select people?" Germany and France both have a great history of heroes and benefactors. So do England and Italy. Let us not forget that the Jews, so dreadfully maligned by Hitler, have rendered immeasurable service to humanity.

In "Mein Kampf," Hitler depicts the life of a typical proletarian family, living in a dismal basement flat where the children are a constant source of dissension between the mother and the father. He tries to point out that the moral barbarism of German youth is attributable to the dreadful social conditions under which it was forced to live. We might expect from this that Hitler would be interested in ameliorating the lot of his compatriots and in sparing them the misery of such a life.

Hitler, however, arrives at curious conclusions. He is provoked by this state of affairs only because people dwelling in such basement flats cannot easily be converted to the "national idea." In his opinion their situation must be improved solely for the purpose of rendering them more easily "nationalized."

I, too, feel that these people should be freed from their dismal haunts and provided with light and airy homes, not to delude them politically but so that they may enjoy life as useful members of society and learn to appreciate others. The very fact that there are such basement flats and that such dreadful economic circumstances prevail denies nationalism, particularly German Nationalism, any basis for its existence. Can Germans struggling bitterly for material needs take pride in the heroic deeds of their ancestors? Of what should these step-children of life be proud? Have their forefathers so provided for them that they have the time and leisure to read about their feats? Does Hitler really believe that he can improve the lot of the worker by bringing national chauvinism to the boiling point? Does not Hitler know that nationalism in every country inevitably leads to war? Would the lot of the basement family be improved if the father of a family were marched off to meet his death in the trenches, or returned a hopeless cripple?

Man by nature leads a gregarious life. Such a life is not self-sufficient but is intended to give the individual greater material, intellectual and spiritual comfort. The closest social life is unquestionably that of the family. Brothers and sisters who live for years in close contact with their parents develop a certain attachment toward one another. After they have left the parental roof they frequently fall into quarrels and drift apart. Yet, where could close ties better develop than in the family? How much weaker and more unnatural is the emphasized feeling of nationality that is based on a much looser society of humans forming the nation? I undoubtedly will be regarded as a heretic by many people; but what I say is true. It seldom has been seen that any creditor, be he of German or French nationality, will treat his poor debtor with indulgence because he happens to be a member of the German or French nation.

There are certain instances in which adherence to a society carries with it a profound interest in the fate of its members. I can well imagine that people who have spent many years together in prison will be concerned about the fate of their former companions even after they themselves have been liberated. I can appreciate also that people who have lain together in the same trenches will manifest an interest in one another in later life. The same is true of people who have gone to school together or have even taken a trip together. In all such cases there is an attachment for those with whom one has experienced a greater or smaller portion of one's life. If the nationalist really feels a passionate love for his own, he should extend this to all individual members of his nation. How could he enjoy his income, his comfort and his wealth if he knew that millions of his extraction were starving, went about in rags or abided in such basements as Hitler so mournfully described? How is it possible for a German who runs down a few Jews or Frenchmen every day at breakfast or at supper, to quietly walk by a poor German beggar whose eyes reflect the tortures of hunger? How is it possible for such nationalists to be traitors and even murderers of their own people? What happened on June 30, 1934? Hundreds of people were torn away and slaughtered without due process of law. Who were these people? They were people whose national-mindedness no one could doubt. They were not from the masses. They were leaders, they were "noble men" who for years had fought by Hitler's side for the national Renaissance. Were they really such rascals that they deserved to be shot like mad dogs? If they were, they do not lend substance to Hitler's statement that nationalists are possessed of strict morality and of sensitivity to social needs. Roehm and Ernst were said to have conducted unnatural orgies in their luxurious villas. What respect can one have for a nationalism whose noblest exponents are mentally diseased? Were they "sensitive to social needs" when they held champagne banquets and lived a life of dissipation while millions of their compatriots were placed on insufficient winter relief? Or were they innocently murdered? In any event, nationalism would have no defense in Germany.

Why did the Nazi henchmen murder General Schleicher and his wife in cold blood? Schleicher was a "German" who had rendered great service to his Fatherland during the War and was a close friend of Hindenburg. Why did they murder Klausener, the Centrist Deputy, who had committed no offense? He, too, was a German whose great devotion to his country was common knowledge.

Why are German Catholics persecuted and intimidated in Germany? Why has such ruthless force been exerted against that noble prince of the Church, Cardinal Faulhaber, who has demonstrated the most admirable courage and deepest moral religiosity in his hour of greatest need? Is not he a German? Are not the many political victims who were dragged into concentration camps, thrown into prisons and murdered ***en masse*** Germans? Why do we not find the slightest trace of sympathy in the treatment of these political opponents who as Germans share the same historical past with Hitler?

The answer to these questions is simple: National Socialism is a gross swindle, a fraud, an invention of diseased and criminal minds that perpetrate a hoax to attain their spurious goals and to satisfy their inconsummate ego. The hymn of nationalism is sung and reverenced as long as it produces political results. As soon as it impels the statesmen abroad to action against Germany, the song is referred to as a phantom or a product of the imagination. Therein lies the disparity between the words and deeds of the nationalists.

Long association with members of various nationalities has taught me to love them for their fine individual characters. Among these friends I count many Germans who would be willing to lay down their lives for the cause of justice. And the same is true of the Czechs, the Poles and the Jews in my acquaintance. They are all respectable and intellectually honest people. I judge my friends by their character, not by their nationality.

Whoever has lived in Austria knows what a chauvinist is. The world has been told how the Austrians long to unite with the Germans. This desire for Anschluss with Germany is greatly exaggerated. In the past various political leaders believed that a union of Austria and Germany would augment their power individually. The Austrian masses had deeper concerns than returning to the "never-to-be-forgotten fatherland." The bourgeois classes were outspoken opponents of Anschluss with Germany and consented to it after the general debacle only with reluctance and under pressure. Only the German-Nationalist students and the old alumni of the nationalistic fraternities desired Anschluss. The Austrian people never wanted to give up their national independence. In later years a German-Austrian Peoples League was founded to prepare the way for Anschluss. It never had any response from the masses. It was only through political duress that they blindly obeyed. When the Entente demanded the secession of Austria from Germany at the Peace Conference, no one in Austria was particularly perturbed.

I believe that it is better to praise a foreign country than one's own. Hitler upbraids the Austrians for perpetuating a cult of Gallic worship before the War. He twists and exaggerates the true facts. A French cult in Germany and a German cult in France would have been much more useful to society than the mutual chauvinistic hatred of these nations, which resulted in a war that caused millions of peoples to lose their lives, their fortunes and their providers.

In the quest for happiness and security the question of nationality plays a subordinate role.

It is only natural for a man to be attached to those who possess the same language and history as he does. The feeling of love for his family and interest in their welfare is more intense than the feeling of nationality. Nationality seldom determines one's material prosperity. Whoever is diligent and industrious can succeed in any country, independent of the color of his hair and eyes and his cephalic index. Intellectual advancement, likewise, does not depend upon nationality. The person who does not cling fanatically to the products of his own nation can enjoy the art and culture of other nations. Can't a German be moved by the music of a foreign composer? Can't he enjoy reading a well-written novel because the author happened to be other than a German?

In describing Vienna, Hitler repeatedly mentions that the city was densely populated by Czechs. In Vienna, as in other parts of Austria, there are many families of non-Germanic descent. The father or the grandfather, the mother or the grandmother may have been Czechs, Hungarians or of other non-Aryan nationalities. Many French immigrants have made their home in Austria.

These foreign elements have assimilated so closely with the German stock that it is scarcely possible to differentiate them. I am acquainted with a certain National Councillor who complies to the strictest requirements for the Nordic type and who speaks a flawless German. When I met his father, I immediately recognized him as a Czech. In fact, the old gentleman made no secret of it.

There are thousands of such families in Vienna. How could Hitler expect these people to long for Anschluss? They could hardly wax enthusiastic about the glorious deeds of the ancient Teutons.

When Hitler began his battle, it never occurred to him that he could find active support among the bourgeoisie. He designated the nationalism of the bourgeoisie as inadequate, but felt that it would offer no resistance to a powerful national policy because of its proverbial cowardice. Hitler did not believe that the masses were naturally sufficiently nationalistic. He says of them: "They will smother every attempt at revolution in Germany as they once stabbed the German army in the back." Here Hitler refers to 15 million people whom he classifies as Marxists, Democrats, Pacifists and Centrists. He feels that all these compatriots "because of their majority number, will hinder every nationalistic political maneuver."

Hitler therefore deemed no sacrifice too great in order to intensify the nationalism of the masses. He believed that during the war the German industrialists should have closely guarded the interests of the German workers and made them every possible concession at any cost whatsoever, created strikes and settled them to the obvious satisfaction of the people, so that they, in turn, would have become fanatical nationalists and would have rallied to the national defense.

Hitler stated that such a radical nationalisation of the masses would have made it impossible to lose the War. "How ridiculous," he writes, "would all the greatest economic concessions have been as opposed to the tremendous significance of a war won."

How little Hitler must think of nationalism if he claims that it could be developed only by generous economic concessions. Germany did not lose the war because the workers were not nationalistic enough, but because her opponents were stronger and because luck was with them. Had the workers struck and left their Fatherland in the lurch during the war it would have been a real stab in the back. Such strikes certainly would not have led to economic concessions but to bloody civil war.

According to the Führer: "The nationalization of the masses can never be achieved by half measures or by a weak emphasis of a so-called objective stand-point, but only by a ruthless and fanatically one-sided presentation of the goal to be achieved. The masses do not consist of professors or of diplomats. They are responsive only to vigor and never to irresolution. They respond better to emotion than to scientific knowledge. Respect induces change quicker than love. Hate lasts longer than antipathy, and the motivating forces of the most powerful revolutions on earth have arisen less from a scientific evaluation of ills than from a fanaticism incited in the masses, and often from a hysteria which impels them forward."

And now Hitler's main premise: "The soul of a people can

be won only by battling for one's goal and by annihilating all opponents to that goal. The people have always recognized that the proof of their own righteousness lies in a ruthless attack against the enemy. They feel that failure to destroy the enemy makes their own rights insecure and places them in the position of being wrong. The masses do not shake hands like people who are friends but admit to opposite interests. What they desire is the victory of the strong and the annihilation or overwhelming defeat of the weak."

How would the Germans have felt had the French proposed such an idea at the Peace Conference? Not very pleased, I assure you. What has National Socialism done for Germany? Germany is the worst hated country in the world. Many countries refuse to buy German goods. German culture has dropped to a medieval level. Have the Nazis improved the lot of the German people, by employing them in factories to fashion ammunition for the next war?

All of Europe is rearming. Since Germany is spending its last cent to build cannons and planes, the other powers are following suit. When rearmament has reached its peak, what will happen to the masses preparing these murderous weapons in the factories? Will millions and millions of people give up their lives on the altar of Nazidom? What can come of such a war? Does Hitler think that Germany will be victorious? Does he not know that were Germany to precipitate the war, France, Italy, England and Russia would mobilise against her?

Germany had been coming to an understanding with her quondam enemies. The able German statesman, Gustav

Stresemann, had concluded a peace pact between Germany and former inimical powers. Germany would have regained some of her colonies if the Nazis had not risen to power.

Dr. Dollfuss, Austria's murdered Chancellor, had political opponents other than the National Socialists. When he appealed to the Austrians to unite against the danger of Anschluss with Germany, opposition disappeared overnight. A storm of enthusiasm broke loose after he proclaimed his campaign for the freedom and independence of Austria. A popular front against Nazism ensued. Even the working classes whose leaders were opposed to Dollfuss joined the fight for Austria's freedom. The Social-Democratic leaders, heretofore always favorably disposed to Anschluss, announced categorically that under no circumstances would they ever consent to Austria's annexation by Germany.

The Nazis have succeeded in nationalizing a portion of the masses. In discussing the nationalization of the masses Hitler points out that, " The greatness of every powerful organization, as an incorporation of an idea, lies in religious fanaticism completely convinced of its own righteousness. When an idea is in itself correct and as such prepares for battle, it is invincible, and thus persecution will only lead to its inner strengthening."

Hitler errs. We must humanize the masses and not dehumanize them through rabid nationalism. If innocent people are being humiliated, tortured and martyred in the concentration camps of Germany, this has become possible through the nationalization of the masses. Religious fanaticism and intolerance will not help the Germans regain their pre-war position. Respect and love for their fellow men, irrespective of belief and nationality, and national reciprocity and cooperation for world peace will more rapidly further this goal.

CHAPTER 3

Race Mania

Hitler realized that not only Germans populate the world; hence he had to find adherents in other countries. In presenting the German people as a superior race apart from others, he would encounter difficulties in spreading his propaganda throughout the world. Therefore, he contrived a ridiculous racial ideology as the keynote of his battle.

Dr. Ladislaus Ajay, a theology professor in Budapest, recently wrote a book called "The Jewish Mirror" in which he established proof of the Jewish descent of some of the leading families, bishops, counts, princes and monarchs of the world. Among the Hungarian families he cites Barons Féhervary and Pronay, Counts Apponyi, Béthlen, Károlyi and Pallavicini, Széchenyi, Teleki and Zichy, and Princes Batthyány, Esterházy, Festetics, Hohenlohe, Palffy and Windischgrätz. Dr. Ajtay found Jewish blood in seventy outstanding noble families of Europe and in the royal families of Greece, Hesse, Italy, Lichtenstein, Monaco and Prussia. He discovered that the Hapsburgs, Bonapartes, Romanoffs and Hohenzollerns are also of Jewish descent. Dr. Ajtay gathered the source material for his book from fifteen years of research in Rome and ten years in Jerusalem. Consequently he took great care not to compromise his life's work by any false references.

Giorgio Pasquali, an Italian journalist, in discussing racial questions recently stated: "I prefer the word nation when I speak of human beings and the word races when I speak of Pekinese, racing horses, chickens and Yorkshire swine .... Who could possibly believe in the purity of modern European races? Anthropologists have proved that racial mixtures go back as far as the Neolithic period. In contemporary Europe, race is a myth. Only the terms nation' and 'fatherland' have a real concept."

Nazi anthropologists classify races into Aryans and non-Aryans. It has been scientifically established that ethnologically there are no Aryans. Even in the earliest days of mankind there must have been differences in people; they could not have been all alike. Those who lived on the sea-coasts must have had an appearance different from those who dwelled in the valleys or in the mountains. Those inhabiting cold climates must have developed physical characteristics different from those in warm climates. People occupied with agriculture must have possessed external characteristics different from hunters and nomads. The same is true today. No two individuals resemble one another in every respect; nor do the members of any given nationality. There is only a white, black, yellow and red race. Physical racial differences are frequently accompanied by psychic differences. These differences do not portend a superiority of one race over another.

No relic portraying the figure of Moses has been handed down to us. Yet his mind and spirit have survived the many centuries. We know that he gave out the Ten Commandments at a time of savagery and barbarity. This man who lived approximately 1,000 years before the birth of Christ should be regarded as one of the outstanding civilizing factors of the world. When through sheer force and strong will he forbade his contemporaries to murder, to steal, to bear false witness and to commit adultery, he rendered immeasurable service to posterity. The color of Moses, eyes and hair bears no importance on his place in world history.

Nero was an Italian and an Aryan. Nero's body has long turned to dust but his evil reputation lives on. Would that he had had a long nose and black kinky hair, but a human soul! It is obviously ridiculous to judge the degree of culture of a race by its corporeal characteristics.

Do we know for certain what our Savior, Jesus Christ looked like? He was certainly no Aryan, but a Semite like Moses. We Catholics and other Christians regard Christ as divine. But even non-Christian confessions who see in Christ only a God-inspired individual, praise his intellectual and spiritual qualities. Can we possibly make the blessing that our Savior brought over the world dependent on the color of his eyes and hair? Hitler's remark that the physically stronger must be victorious applies only to animals, not to human beings.

I understand why people raise pure-blooded dogs or horses whose only significance in life is their physical perfection, but I could never understand stupid attempts to pair off people merely because they possess similar physical characteristics. Imagine a lad, slender as a reed with beautiful blonde hair, beaming blue eyes and a lovely Greek nose, whose soul is as black as the night. According to Hitler, if this person were to marry a Jewess, a crime against nature would have been committed. No matter how beautiful, how strong and how sterling her character, Hitler would disapprove of this marriage, because any children borne of it would be "inferior." Not the father, says Hitler, but the Jewish mother would be to blame for the inferior progeny. Could anything be more absurd?

Marriage should be denied only to sick people. I advocate the breeding of healthy individuals as opposed to the selective breeding of a specific race.

The well-known French Senator, Henri Beranger, recently published an article on the race problem. He wrote — "I read Hitler's 'Mein Kampf' and also National Socialism' by Dr. Goebbels, the present German Minister of Propaganda. When Dr. Goebbels was in Genf, I asked him why he wished to exterminate the Jews and particularly what he had against the German Jews. His answer was — 'They are not Aryans.' Furthermore, the minister remarked, that they participated too much in public life. Those were objections to the blood and to the number of Jews. He could not, however, find any real objections; he could not state that the Jews had bad customs, that they acted inimically to the interests of the State. All in all, he could not present the slightest reason to justify the horrible persecution of the Jews in Germany. Dr.

Goebbels gave me the following statistical data: 'From 40% to 70% of the professions were dominated by the Jews. At first I questioned the authenticity of the statistics. I asked him whether the same difficulties also applied to the Saxons, the Würtemberger and the Silesians. Dr. Goebbels answered, The Würtemberger are Aryans and the Jews are not. The Jews are non-Aryan. Therefore, we have drawn up exceptional laws for them.' I repeated this sentence to a large gathering in Paris. The answer of the public was self-evident — derisive laughter.

"All right, well say the Jews are not Aryans. What of it? What is an Aryan? Is he a blonde, slender person with blue eyes and light skin? Is he small, black-haired, with black eyes, and dark' skinned like Dr. Goebbels? Is Dr. Goebbels an Aryan? The Nazis would say—'Read your own countryman, Count Gobineau!' It is quite difficult for a Frenchman to read Gobineau, for his French is sometimes more difficult than that of a foreigner. Nevertheless, I have read Gobineau, a prophet in a foreign country, for he is certainly not one in his own. From Gobineau I learned that the races of mankind are not equal. The highest place, he says, belongs to the Aryans and the greatest of all Aryans are the Germans.

"I have since learned from the same Gobineau that the Germans are not the Germani, for the Germani, the original inhabitants of modern Germany, were driven out by the Huns, Teutons and Celts. Pure Germans, Gobineau teaches, can only be found in Scotland and in Scandinavia. As for the Germans in Germany, they are a typically mixed race. My reading of Gobineaus work was particularly interesting when I learned that the Aryan blood in its purest form is retained by the Semites, for the Semites are a race that mixed least with others.

"In France," concludes Senator Beranger, "racial problems are negligible. When in the year 1791 the National Assembly proclaimed the emancipation of the Jews, it held that the value of a person is in keeping with his moral and intellectual services. Ernst Renan wrote—'The greatest work of the 19th Century was the destruction of the Ghetto'."

At the peak of its power, the Semitic race was highly accomplished. It excelled in all fields of human endeavor. If the Semites had given us only a Moses and a Jesus, they would have completely fulfilled their cultural mission. They gave us great military leaders; Hannibal was a Semite. The Chaldeans, the Assyrians, the Babylonians and the Phoenicians were Semites. The Semitic peoples were among the first heralds of culture. The Aryans flourished only after the Semites had already played their role in world history. The Greeks, Romans and Germans borrowed much of their culture from the Semites. They enlarged upon these cultural entities with the aid of discoveries and inventions and thus brought humanity to heights previously unattained.

What do the Nazis mean by "heralds of culture?" Do they mean those who incite the worst in people by lies and calumnies, fanaticism and intolerance and turn them loose like wild beasts to destroy and ***exterminate*** others with a bestiality found only in the jungles of Africa? Can individuals be designated as heralds of culture to whom love of neighbor is a foreign phrase, who can never forgive and forget, who aim to destroy all who are not of the same nation or the same state of mind?

Are the Storm Troopers who torture and humiliate their prisoners in the concentration camps of Germany heralds of culture? Did the Nazis offer proof of their advanced culture when in a single night, without investigation and without due process of law, they slaughtered hundreds of people, among them many of their most faithful adherents in times of adversity, merely because these unfortunates stood in their way?

In discussing culture and race purity Hitler states: 'As long as the Aryan ruthlessly upheld the doctrine of rank, he was not only master but guardian and propagator of culture, for culture was based exclusively on his capabilities and thereby on his self-respect. As soon as the conquered people began to rise and assumed the language of their conquerors, a sharp-wall arose between lord and vassal. The Aryan gave up the purity of his blood and thereby lost access to the Paradise that he himself had created. He deteriorated in the racial mixture. He constantly lost more and more of his cultural entities. For a while he could live on accumulated cultural values but torpidity set in and finally ended in oblivion.

"Thus," Hitler writes, "did the cultures and kingdoms collapse to make way for new structures. Blood mixture is the one cause of the demise of all cultures. People do not deteriorate because of wars they have lost, but because of the loss of all power of resistance which is only the property of pure blood."

I take exception to Hitler's facts, and formulas. In the first place, it is not true that the Aryans were the first guardians of culture. Civilization existed thousands of years before the Aryans appeared in history. In the 1928 edition of his "History of the World," H. G. Wells claims that in primitive times and even later, people were differentiated not according to blood but according to language. People who fall within the Indo-European linguistic group are not necessarily related by race. The same is true of people who belong to the Semitic or Mongoloid linguistic group.

The first people to build real cities in any part of the world were probably the Sumerians, people of unknown origin. They were definitely not Aryans. Their capitol, Eridu, was built around 6500 B. C. They made their fields bear fruit by irrigating them with artificial water ditches. They had kine, donkeys, sheep and goats. They built tower-like temples for their religion. They possessed no stones, and consequently sun-dried clay played an important role in their lives. They built with bricks, made pottery and earthenware objects dart and drew and wrote on thin brick-like clay tablets. They were not acquainted with paper or parchment. For 4.000 years the Sumerians were free from subjugation to any foreign people. During this time they were able to develop their civilization, their cuneiform script and their navigation.

At the height of the Sumerian empire certain Semitic-speaking nomadic stocks, who for centuries had engaged in commerce with the Sumerians, now fell upon them. The Semitic nomads attacked and plundered in Sumeria but were eventually driven out. Finally a great leader arose among these Semites. His name was Sargon and he lived 2,500 years before Christ. Sargon united his Semitic nomads, the Akkadians, and conquered the Sumerians. He ruled over a vast realm reaching as far west as the Mediterranean, which was called the Sumerian-Akkadian empire. Although the Akkadians conquered the Sumerian cities, the advanced Sumerian culture won out against the simpler Akkadian culture. The intruders learned the Sumerian language and writing, just as the barbarian peoples of the Middle Ages in Europe learned Latin as the language of knowledge. Thus, as opposed to Hitler's contention, the conquerors took over the culture of the conquered.

This Sumerian-Akkadian empire finally experienced the same fate of all sedentary peoples. From the east came the Elamites and from the west the Amorites. The Elamites were of unknown race and language. Their capitol was Susa. They were certainly not Aryans. The Amorites were Semites of the same strain as Abraham and the later Hebrews. Therefore, before the Aryans even appeared on the surface of world history the forefathers of modern Jewry had already conquered a great empire. These Amorites became the rulers of all Mesopotamia under Hammurabi, one of the most illustrious figures in ancient history. After a century of peace and security, new nomads came from the east and over-flooded Babylonia. They brought with them the horse and chariot and set up their own kingdom in Babylonia. They were the Cassites.

The Amorites were not the only Semites bent on conquest. The Assyrians, a Semitic people, brought their military art to a high level. When they became acquainted with the horse and the war chariot, they conquered Babylonia under Tiglath Pileser I, in 1100 B. C. For many centuries power wavered between Ninevah and Babylon. Some times it was an Assyrian, other times a Babylonian who declared himself "king of the world."

In 606 B. C. a new nomadic tribe of Semites, the Chaldeans, aided by two Aryan people, the Medes and the Persians, took Ninevah. The Persians came from the woods and plains of the north and the northwest. Up to this time the nomadic besiegers of the Assyrians were the Elamites and the Semites. Now the role of conqueror fell to the Aryans for 600 years.

Thus 2,000 years before Christ the Semites had already established great empires. These Semites left a magnificent literature to posterity; the Nimrod Saga is world-renowned. These mighty empires lasted for centuries due to their strict military discipline and subordination. Science and art flourished under the Semites. Greek art was strongly influenced by the Assyrians, as evidenced by recent excavations.

Babylonia contributed much sustenance to that powerful structure known as civilization. As that famous historian, Fritz; Hommel, states in his "History of Babylonia": "From Babylonia the stream of culture went by sea with the Phoenicians and by land over Asia Minor to Greece and

Rome, and thereby eventually to the Roman-Germanic empire."

The Chaldeans taught the western world astronomy and mathematics. The Phoenicians were the founders of navigation. The first boats, to be sure, were constructed early in history by those who dwelled along rivers and lakes but real ships were first built by the Phoenicians. Carthage was a Phoenician colony, and so were numerous colonies in Cyprus, Rhodes, Malta, Sicily, Sardinia, along the north coast of Africa and in southern Spain. Purple dies, weaving, manufacture of glass, mining, metallurgy and architecture were partly discovered and partly advanced by the Phoenicians. The Phoenicians awakened a mercantile sense in the Greek. From the Phoenicians the Greeks learned to steer their course at night by the North Star. In the face of all this Hitler has the audacity to state that the Semites had no talent for art, technical discovery, navigation and colonization. Were the Phoenicians an "inferior race"?

Coudenhove-Kalergi in his book, "Das Wesen des Antisemitismus" (The Essence of Anti-Semitism), states that "The Semites were highly civilized when the Aryans were still wild animals. Babylonia is not only the mother of Semitic, Grecian and Roman culture, but the mother of the entire Occident and therefore of our culture. Besides Babylonia there are only two civilizations that deserve the name culture, and they are the Indian and the Chinese. Babylonian culture was very extensive and very profound."

The word Aryan is only a linguistic term. The greatest and

the most famous authority on Aryanism, Professor Max Müller, declared that: "Aryan is a technical expression designating one of a large family of languages ranging from India to northern Europe. Just as the term Semitic is purely linguistic, so is the term Aryan the same. A century ago the world knew nothing of a racial difference between Aryans and Semites."

Civilization was basically founded by the Sumerians, a non-Aryan people, and was later advanced by the Semites. Human culture was at least 6,000 years old before the Aryans made their debut on the stage of history.

But the Reichsführer maintains that: "What we regard today as human culture, as the sum of art, science and technology, is the exclusive creative product of the Aryan. This fact permits us to conclude that he alone was the founder of higher humanity and consequently is the prototype of him whom we understand by the word 'man.' He is the Prometheus of humanity from whom sprang the light of the stars, the divine spark of genius, which repeatedly lights the fire that illuminates the night of silent mysteries, and thus allows man to ascend the way to rule the other beings of this earth. If the Aryan is ousted, pitch darkness after thousands of years of light will again descend upon the earth. Human culture will die and the world will sink into oblivion."

Hitler ought to study world history. Were the Sumerians, Assyrians, Babylonians, Chaldeans and the Phoenicians to rise from their graves, they would rightfully remind him that without their religions and without their accomplishments in the field of art and science, the peoples of the world would find it impossible to cite the achievements of which they are so very proud. The Sumerians would point to their development of agriculture, the Assyrians, the Babylonians and the Chaldeans to their wonderful organized armies, their architecture and their poetry, the Phoenicians to their navigation, their progress in grammar, arithmetic and astronomy, all of which forms the sum total of knowledge upon which Occidental culture is based. The proscribed Jews should also remind Hitler that Christ was a Jew, that he taught the religion of "love thy neighbor," that Moses was also a Jew and that a thousand years ago, in his Ten Commandments, he had prohibited murder, covetousness, theft, adultery and the bearing of false witness. Therefore, when Hitler claims that the Aryans alone were the founders of higher culture and that they represent the prototype of that which we understand by the word man, he is completely and voluntarily misinformed.

chapter 4

Racial Characteristics of the Jews

The racial theories of the Nazis are as fraudulent and stupid as their other teachings. They do not realize that there are inferior and superior individuals in every race. The Jews do not comprise a race, nor do they all possess the same racial characteristics. A pure race does not exist. Only the Australian Bushmen, the Hottentots and some African Negrito tribes are comparatively racially pure. Aside from groups distinguished by the color of their skin, if the term race is to be applied, the Jews, like the Germans, are a racial mixture.

Wilser, a nationalistic racial investigator, in his "Ancient Germans" maintains that: "Only a small percentage of our people has the measurement and body structure of the skeletons of the German migration period. If we really want to find Germanic stock, we must turn to our northern cousins, the Swedes, the Dutch and the English."

Dr. Fritz Lens, the famous authority on Eugenics, says in his "Menschliche Erblichkeitslehre" (Doctrine of Human Heredity, 3rd edition, 1927, page 365) that: "It should not be overlooked that both (the Jews and the Germans) are very similar in essential abilities; and this is even true if by Germans, we mean only those individuals of preponderantly Nordic stock. Naturally, there are differences between races but they are not insurmountable. I must dispute the argument that one race is inferior to another."

Professor Lenz goes on to say: "The differences between various racial predispositions are less than the differences between normal and diseased predispositions. The hereditary substance of most people is so commingled that it is impossible to estimate the respective portions of each race in an individual," (Bauer, Fischer and Lenz—"Grundrisse der menschlichen Erblichkeitslehre und Rassen'Hygiene," 3rd edition, 1927, pages 521 and 573, (Foundations of the Doctrine of Human Heredity and Race Hygiene).

According to Felix von Luschan, Director of the Berlin Anthropological Museum, all of humanity consists of one single species, there is no such thing as an inferior race and the differences between races, particularly those affecting moral characteristics and intelligence, are not as great as the differences between individuals of the same race.

Different investigators may have contradictory opinions about a race. Dr. Ernst Kretschmer, Professor of Psychiatry and Neurology at Marburg, claims that the task of evaluating a race is "almost always selected and carried out so one-sidedly and tendenciously that it gives the impression of a caricature. Race theses are written to give the author an opportunity to glorify his own race or to treat his own political tendencies and idealistic dreams with pseudo-scientific means." In "Geniale Menschen", pages 73 and 74, Kretschmer says that: "One seeks the best in his own race and the worst in others, depicting only the positive virtues of the one and the negative qualities of the other . . ."

Among the German savants strongly opposed to anti-Semitism were Alexander von Humboldt, Bär, Virchow, Kollman, Ranke, Luschan, Bals, Buckle; Bott, Müller and Graber, the founders of the Indo-Germanic linguistic system; Ihering, the famous law teacher; F. Müller and Ratzl, the ethnologists; Nietzsche, Wilhelm Wundt, Theobald Ziegler and E. von Aster, the philosophers; Pensig and Jodl, the moralists; Weber and Muller-Lyer, the sociologists, and others. Jodl finds that "no more ominous insanity is conceivable and nothing must be more opposed than that which makes moral good or moral evil the alleged hereditary property of a given race." V. Suk, a well-known physician and philosopher, and professor of Anthropology and Folk-lore at Masaryk University in Prague, calls attention in his "Rasse und Moderne Forschung" (Race and Modern Investigation) to 3,000 precipitation experiments conducted on the blood of Jews, so-called Nordics, Alpines, Baltics and members of other European races, Eskimos, Kalmuks and Gypsies. He states, "We found that the blood of Jews, Nordics and others was not clearly differentiated while the difference between the blood of Eskimos and Europeans was marked. The Kalmuks and Eskimos, having common physical characteristics, showed related blood reactions. Just as we have previously objected to the usage of the term race, do we object to the terms Aryan and Jewish. Scientifically the term

Aryan denotes members of certain people whose languages and some ofwhose cultural entities are traceable to a common origin. Thus the Gypsies are Aryans just as much as the Germans. Biologically the term Jewish has as much value as the term Aryan. It does not denote a race. Historical, archaeologic, ethnologic and biologic research has proved that Jews possess proto-Asiatic, Dinaric, Oriental, Mediterranean and Nordic traits . . . Our experiments on the blood serum of various types of Jews when compared with the sera of Europeans, show no essential differences, whereas when both are compared with the sera of Eskimos, great differences are observed ... The Jews have many physical characteristics which are the property of other racial groups. If the race anthropologists find from ten to twenty races among the Europeans, just as many races can be found among the Jews. Place a photograph of a black-haired, black-eyed Jew from North Africa beside that of a red-headed blue-eyed Jew from Carpatho-Russia, then a few photographs of Italian and French Jews, and to make the difference more apparent, several photographs of English Jews, and you will have to agree with me that Jewish is a term that has nothing to do with the biological conception of race. It could be stated inversely that the Nordics possess many Jewish traits. If we go from the biological to the ethnological, psychological and cultural interpretation of the term Jewish, the same confusion enters the picture . . ."

In his "Rassenkunde des Judischen Volkes" (Racial Science of the Jewish People), Munich, 1929, Hans F. K. Günther resorts to unscientific, one-sided and inadequate material. According to Günther, the Jews are differentiated from other races not as one race from another but as one racial mixture from other combined racial mixtures. Thus, he finds, that it is not the "inferiority" of the Jewish racial mixture that constitutes the core of the Jewish question, but rather its being racially of a different type; above all, it is a racially psychic foreignness amidst the various Occidental peoples. Günther defines the Jewish spiritual morale as very low because the core of the Jewish spirit is formed from the character features of a proto-Asiatic race. Günther denies the Jews the ability to speak correct German. Yet, Gundolf, one of the greatest masters of the German language, was a Jew. How does Günther reconcile this?

It is most interesting to learn from Günther that the Jews also are descended from the eulogized Nordic race and the old Amorites and Philistines. In referring to the talented and important representatives of modern Jewry, Günther remarks that they owe their genius to their Nordic mixture.

Professor Müller-Freienfels in his "Psychologie des Deutschen Menschen und Seiner Kultur" (Psychology of the German and His Culture), page 230, declares that . . . "Even where there was no racial mixture but only a cultural Germanization of the Jews, it could not be denied that many Jews were worthy representatives of the German esprit. The 'folk itself has rendered favorable judgment insofar as it regards the music of Mendelsohn and the poetry of Heine as Lieder (folk-songs)."

According to Houston Stewart Chamberlain in his "Foundations of the 19th Century", Munich, 1919—page

496, the racial characteristics of the true German are "large, beaming, heavenly eyes, gigantic stature, blonde hair, long musculature, long head and a noble countenance." Investigations conducted among German school children showed 31-8% to be pure blondes with blue and grey eyes, 14-1% brunettes with dark eyes and hair and 54-1% mixed nondescript types. Even Dr. Günther asserts that only 10% of the inhabitants of Germany are Nordic. Maurice Fishberg in his "Rassenmerkmale der Jüden" (Racial Characteristics of the Jews), Munich, 191 3, states that of 4,120 Jews studied, 37% of the men and 59% of the women had straight, sometimes Greek noses, while only from I 3 to 14% approximated the so-called Jewish type.

Privy Councillor V Gruber, President of the Bavarian Academy of Sciences, and a member of the nationalistic Pan-German League, analyzed Hitler's features in the "Essener Volkswacht" of November 9, 1929: "For the first time I saw Hitler from close. His face and head indicated a poor race, a hybrid ... low, receding, forehead, ugly nose, high cheekbones, small eyes, dark hair; a little brush of a mustache, only as wide as his nose, gives a challenging appearance to his face. His facial expression is not that of one in complete control of his senses but of an aroused lunatic ... constant twitching of the facial muscles; an expression of great self-satisfaction."

The "folk" theory contends that an Aryan does not have to be educated to a rejection of products of the Jewish mind; this instinct is supposed to be in his blood. Therefore, whoever still errs, has not yet achieved inner perfection. The stupidity of such contentions is illustrated by the following examples:

In issue 270 of the "Freiheits Kampf ' for 1921, Phillip Jantschner, an architect, reviled modern architecture in an article entitled "A Taste of Desolation". "... What does horizontalism mean to us Germans? A denial of life, a mind picture of the night, of rest, of decline and of the destruction of all forces moving upward. When in 1905 the elder architect, Alfred Messel, completed the Wertheim Building in Berlin, a new height was reached in German architecture. Many architects, consciously or unconsciously, copied this reminiscence of the Gothic, the German style."

Alfred Messel is a Jew. Even the "folk" theorists cannot deny that his style is German. Did they not know his descent, or can't they think with their blood any more?

Heinrich Klass, a Pan-Germanist, glorified the Wertheim Building as a symbol of modern German architecture in his "German History ", Leipzig, 1914- When he found out that Messel was of Jewish descent, this passage was omitted from the next edition of his book. Did the Wertheim Building lose its beauty between both editions?

The chauvinistic "Deutsche Tageszeitung" of July I, 1911, reported the following on Friedrich Gundolf's work, "Shakespeare und der Deutsche Geist', obviously unaware that Gundolf, born Gunthelfinger, was a Jew: "A very deft esprit permeates the whole, a deep self effacing reverence for everything great and beautiful, a rare nobility of mind, aristocracy of soul and of reason. We have once more received a masterpiece of German genius."

At the 1928 Olympics in Amsterdam, Helene Mayer of Offenbach won the world's championship in foil-fencing. The nationalistic newspaper "Fridericus" of Hamburg extolled Miss Mayer to the nth degree of Aryan sublimity: "Hats off to this blonde German girl, who amidst the black-haired international mishpochoh that strived to set the fashion in Amsterdam, remained true to her German allegiance and wore the betrayed and proscribed black, white and red." In her first victorious bout, Fräulein Mayer wore the colors of her fencing club which happened to be black, white and red.

The most amusing fact is that the blue-eyed, blonde Helene Mayer was the daughter of a Jewish physician and was, therefore, a German Jewess. After Hitler's seizure of power, Helene Mayer had to leave Germany because she was excluded from all sport events and competitive bouts.

Robert von Lieben, the inventor of the radio tube, was praised by the nationalistic German press as a German inventor who embodied all the Germanic virtues. "Fridericus" (Nov. 3, 1930) reported: "If you want to know the real inventor and improver of the electron tube, he is the German, Baron von Lieben; and whether it pleases Jewry or not, we are quite ready once and for all to make public the way in which the Jewish Telegraphic Agency treated this German pioneer . . . and how it managed to acquire the valuable patents of Baron von Lieben which today are of basic importance to radio technology."

Again "Fridericus" was wrong, for Baron von Lieben was a Viennese Jew.

Fishberg studied the physical features of a vast number of Jews. He emphatically denies the existence of a single uniform type of Jew. A great number of Jewish types strongly approximate the general type of the peoples among whom they live. The Jews of Germany, for example, resemble other Germans much more than the Jews of Russia or of Palestine. In Jerusalem among the children of the Ashkenazim, 40% are blonde and 30% blue-eyed, while 10% of the Sephardic children are blonde. Virchow found that of 75,000 Jewish children in Germany 32% had light hair, 46% light eyes, while in Austria 28% had light hair and 54% light eyes. In Fishberg's cases only a small minority possessed the so-called Jewish nose; 57% and 59% of the Jewesses had Grecian noses and 13% of all cases had hooked noses. Were many of the Polish Jews to cut off their beards and temple locks and don European clothes, they would present a surprisingly Nordic appearance.

Jews were excluded from agriculture, industry and trade during the Middle Ages. They could exist only by selling old clothes or by engaging in money businesses. Whoever wished to be freed from these ugly professions had to be an important man. Many Jews succeeded, nevertheless, in devoting themselves to scientific professions. It is indicative of great genius that they were able to penetrate the walls of the Ghetto and attain high positions with various monarchs and popes. The greater number of Jews, however, was doomed to a life in the dark Ghetto where they sharpened their wits by studying Hebraic literature.

The Nazis deprecate the unusual keenness of mind and critical ability of the Jews. The Jewish mind was spurred on to perfection by the behavior of the Gentiles. Training is the most important factor in the development of skill and talent. The Jews were not limited intellectually to their professions. In the Ghetto it was customary for the father of the family to take care of all of his dependents, even the older children who were able to support themselves. Thus many Jews made use of their time to solve the most difficult and complicated religious problems and to engage in sagacious dialogues and fiery debates. These battles constituted excellent training for the Jewish mind. These mental faculties did not die out but were passed on from generation to generation.

When the gates of the Ghetto were thrown open, the Jews applied their skill to the professions and their keenness of mind to the solutions of other problems. Here they met with the resistance of their non-jewish competitors. It was not only economic jealousy that gave birth to this new feeling of enmity for the Jew. Some Christians could not abide these "inferior individuals" who only yesterday wore the Jewish badge of shame and did not dare sit beside them in the university, practice as physicians in the hospitals, act as attorneys in the courts and take for granted the same rights in public life as other people. Had a miracle occurred that would have enabled the Jews to adapt their appearance, behavior, gestures, speech, movements and manners to their immediate environment, the opposition might not have been so harsh. Generations had to pass before this process of assimilation could be completed. In the meantime there were always despicable creatures who took advantage of innocent Jews. Finally the Jews could not tend to their businesses and some had to revert to usury and money-lending. Their enemies used this excuse to incite the masses against them.

The Jews were naive enough to believe that their emancipation from the Ghetto was due to the sympathy of their Christian brethren. In reality, it was only the logical result of the many revolutions that they should be guaranteed human rights. But the emancipation of the Jews could not erase the religious prejudice or inherited antipathy from the hearts of the people. Thus the Jews remained burdened with the stigma of the Ghetto. They were subjected to the constant envy of their Gentile competitors and to the hatred of the fanatical and ignorant masses aroused by the anti-Semites. They lacked a resolute leader in their newly acquired freedom.

As long as there are Jews who continue to lead an unhealthy and uncultivated type of life, which has nothing to do with the Jewish religion or with Zionism, the enemies of the Jews will use them as scapegoats for the crimes of others. The Ghetto was a serious illness for the Jewish people. Its after-effects have not yet been completely wiped out; would it not be better to cure them rather than breed them artificially? In Palestine every trace of Ghetto mentality has been obliterated. These humiliated and frightened creatures of Eastern Europe have been transformed into sturdy and industrious farmers. The smell of their own soil has accomplished this miracle. Their children look like the sons and daughters of farmers all over the world. A healthy Jewish laboring class is flourishing in Palestine. In the factories Jewish workers conscientiously participate in the production of wares.

Palestine is becoming a paradise, exclusively through the efforts of the Jews, the same Jews who were always reviled as parasites, as sensual, rapacious and materialistic people devoid of all idealism. These Jews have reclaimed Palestine at the cost of life and health. They have converted a once dismal and sparsely settled land into a bright, fertile, well populated country. Where once jackals growled, the happy singing of the Jewish workers is heard. Just as in ancient Judea when the prophets were artisans, manual labor is in high regard in the Palestine of today. Jews who were professional men or students in Germany two years ago now work in the fields and factories. Jewish young ladies who formerly had been devotees of teas and musicales now look after the cattle and plant vegetables.

In a recent sermon Cardinal Faulhaber said: "When several months ago I arose against the inhuman racial hatred activated by a clique of our German brethren, they wanted to stone me. My life was in danger but I was not afraid, for I acted from the deepest conviction. The Jews are persecuted all over the world, but the methods of persecution in our country are a shame and a disgrace to us. History has taught that God always punishes the tormentors of the Jewish people. When on June 30th God punished some of the tormentors of the Jews, no Catholic felt sorry for them. Their punishment was well deserved. Catholics, brothers! Don't you see that this was a chastisement from God? The Jews will not be exterminated by hatred and persecution. The oldest people in the world has already gone through much suffering. They suffer now and will always suffer because they have remained true to their great faith. We must honor and esteem them for they have given the world the most glorious and invaluable gift—the Bible. Enlighten your brothers, tell them that racial hatred is a wild and poisonous growth in our life. Eradicate from your hearts this dreadful and inhuman prejudice against the eternal suffering people."

Official French headquarters recently issued a news dispatch to the effect that "rumors that legal or administrative steps will be taken against Jewish immigrants in France are being circulated abroad by anti-Semitic sources. There is absolutely no basis for these rumors. Not a single legal measure has or will be directed against Jews, native or otherwise. Anti-Semitic discrimination does not exist in France."

The former Premier and present Minister of France, Edouard Herriot, made the following statement to a New York newspaper: "The Jews have completely assimilated with the French people. They cooperate loyally in every matter. Their sons lost their lives on the battle-fields with our sons, not only during the last war but during every war since the emancipation of the Jews by the French National Assembly of 1789. French culture has been enriched by Jewish contributions. For this we are thankful to the Jews. The people and organizations who attempt to split the French nation on the racial question are playing with fire. Because the essence of democracy is tolerance, such people have been tolerated. But, we will sharply resist any sabotage to our democratic principles, and we shall never allow our Jewish citizens to be humiliated as they are in other countries. If reaction goes from words to deeds it will strike up against the firm resistance of a great radical majority of the French people which will protect the ideals of liberty, equality and fraternity not only with words but with blood. Jews form an organic part of our society. Whoever disturbs them attacks the sovereignty of the French people."

Dr. Milner of Belfast tells us that "no single race is perfect and for every Jewish criminal, there are at least two non-Jewish criminals in proportion to the respective population. Jews today are undeservedly the victims of economic, political and social bans; civilization is greatly to be blamed for the plight of the Jews. It is a fact worthy of notice that Jew-less nations usually sink to an inferior position. Spain is such an example . . . Jews are always a valuable element in the fatherlands of their choice. They are outstanding in commerce and only by commerce can countries exist. Statistics on criminals prove that Jews are more law-abiding than their Christian neighbors and thereby set a good example. To total abstainers it may be of interest to know that unbridled love of alcohol is rarely found among Jews. The highest type of Jew is cultured, intelligent and possesses great respect for human values."

In the course of an address before the Czech Parliament, President Masaryk remarked: "I am convinced that whoever accepts Jesus as his spiritual leader can never be an anti-Semite . . . because Jesus himself was a Jew, because the Apostles were Jews and because orthodox Christianity, particularly Catholicism, is based on Judaism. If I accept Jesus,

I cannot be an anti-Semite. You must be one or the other—a Christian or an anti-Semite—you cannot be both!"

When the French National Assembly met in 1789 to discuss the Edict of Tolerance for the Jews, Count Mirabeau arose and cried out in a thundering voice that reverberated through the room: "Tolerance? I don't want to hear that ugly word any more! It is not tolerance but fraternity, complete fraternity that I demand!

National Socialist propaganda often attempts to link the great German minds of the past with Hitler. I'm afraid this has not met with great success. Before Hitler "saved Germany, this nation of poets and thinkers had views entirely different from those of the present rulers of the Third Reich. There is a yawning abyss between the universalistic, humanitarian genius of Goethe or Lessing and what is known as culture in Germany of today. Such literary titans as Goethe and Lessing are avoided by the Nazis, but in Friedrich Nietzsche they think they have found a real precursor of National Socialism.

Would Nietzsche have been a Nazi? I doubt it. When Theodore Fritsch, editor of the anti-Semitic newspaper, "Der Hammer", wanted to convince Nietzsche of the authenticity of the racial theory and the consequent justification for anti-Semitism, he tried to influence him via continuous correspondence. This became too much for Nietzsche, and one day he answered the zealous race missionary as follows:

(I am quoting from two letters of Nietzsche which were published in the "Neuen Tagbuch").

Nice, France, March 23, 1887.

"... Objectively speaking, the Jews are much more interesting to me than the Germans; their history deals with fundamental problems. I confess, furthermore, that I feel so untouched by the present German 'esprit' that I cannot regard its idiosyncrasies with much patience. Among these, I count the oddity of anti-Semitism. Oh! If you only knew how much I laughed last spring over the books of that sentimental square-head whose name is Paul Lagarde."

Nice, France, April 29, 1887.

"... I asked you kindly not to remember me any more with such missiles. I fear that my patience is at an end. You may believe me that this nauseating intrusion of naive dilettantes to have their say as to the value of peoples and races, this submission to 'authorities' who have been avoided with cold disdain by everyone in possession of his own mental faculties, these constant absurd falsifications and trimmings of the terms Germanic, Semitic, Aryan, will all permanently enrage me and will deprive me of the ironic good nature with which I have hitherto regarded the virtuous Pharisees among the present Germans . . . , and finally, how do you think I feel when the name Zarathustra is used in the mouths of anti-Semites?"

In his "Zur Geneologie der Moral" Nietzsche says: "How much mendacity and infamy is used in discussing the racial question in the European mixture of today! (It has recently been established that man did not have his origin in Borneo but in Horneo). Resolution:—Not to go around with anyone who has taken part in this foolhardy race swindle."

Nietzsche claims in his "Frohliche Wissenschaft" that: "Europe owes the Jews no small thanks for its development of logic and habits of reason . . . The Jews in modern Europe have graced upon the highest form of intellectualism."

I am positive that Friedrich Nietzsche would have despised the author of "Mein Kampf'. The Nietzchean realm of the superman is one of intellect always progressing further and further. It would have excluded such limited minds as Adolf Hitler. A man who reproves another as sub-human and who is himself a product of barbarity is certainly no superman in the sense of the author of Zarathustra. Nietzsche's ideal, moreover, was "the good European". Racial or national arrogance he considered "duffer nationalism". He had a strong instinctive dislike for duress and tyranny.

In August of 193 3 the Central News Agency issued a report on the attitude of Pope Pius XI toward the anti-Semitic movement in Germany. The pontiff declared that the persecution of the Jews is a sign of poverty in the civilization of a great people. He also mentioned that Jesus Christ, the Mother of God, and her family, the Apostles and many Saints were Jews and that the Bible was the creation of the Jews. The Aryan peoples, he said, had no claim to superiority over the Semites.

Karin Michaelis, the famous Danish authoress and humanitarian, wrote the following about the unfortunate situation of the German Jews. "Yes, this Jewish question has caused me many a sleepless night and I still see no way out. It seems so improbable and so inhumane that in this era such a thing could be possible. For me this is especially hard to believe because since my early childhood and adolescence, my dearest friends have been Jews, and I treasure these friendships today. We in Denmark, thank God, know no Jewish question. We are too civilized to allow anything like that to happen. Many Jewish families who have lost position, money and every thing in Germany have come to me. They brought their small charming children along with them. I always think: Shouldn't these children be enough to stop that persecution? The parents are pale, their hands tremble and their eyes are filled with tears. Nothing can be done other than to offer them a little shelter. They remind me of lepers. Innocent they are, and into exile they have been driven. What good is it that they are allowed to leave Germany when no work is offered to them abroad? Are we not all brothers? Do they really believe in Germany, where most of the people are pious and God-fearing, that Almighty God could have been so unjust as to allow people to come into the world without granting them a spot on the surface of the earth and the right to live among other people? Why don't the heavens open so that Germany's men and women will finally hear the divine word and learn how very grievously they err!

"How can little Nazi children be taught to be good and decent persons, to harm neither flora nor fauna, when simultaneously human beings are being disfranchised in Germany? Oh, those little Jewish children! They gaze with astonishment at their parents. 'What have you done, what is wrong with us?' The treatment of the Jews is as dreadful for the Aryan children as it is for the Jewish children; for the Aryan children laden their souls with sins and these sins cannot be wiped out. What is very touching is that not one Jewish refugee has demonstrated an unholy rage against Germany. A shrug of the shoulders. That is all. And even today these outcasts still love the German soil in which their fathers and forefathers lay buried.

"It is just this resignation to fate that makes it so dreadful, so impossible for us bystanders to understand. Don't I know how during the war the Jewish doctors gave up their last bit of energy and flirted with death to aid the wounded? Haven't I seen Jewish women give up man and child for the Fatherland, lose everything and quietly and oh, so nobly assume their places as nurses, without complaints and without fuss? Oh, I am so unhappy, so bitter, because I know the Jewish race, because I love and honor it. What more can I say? Every people claims that it is hospitable . . . But where is there such hospitality as 'My home is your home'? If such a phenomenon only existed, I could lay quiet and fall asleep."

In 1928 Eduard Lamporter, the City Chaplain of Stuttgart, published "Das Judentum in seiner kulturund religions-geschichtlichen Erscheinung" (Judaism in its Historical, Cultural and Religious Manifestation). This monumental work, whose author "was impelled by a motive to rectify a wrong perpetrated against Jewry on German soil since the seventh century ", combats the fantastic lies of racial propaganda with real facts and simple clear scientific data. The author, a servant of God, is likewise a servant of truth.

To the world of hatred and low passions he cries out—"Truth is the greatest enemy of anti-Semitism!"

"The German Jews have made their home on German soil for more than one thousand years. We are closely tied to them by fate. Throughout the centuries they have shared joy and sorrow, fortune and misfortune with the German people. Have we any right to reject and attack them as a foreign impure race, and to exclude ourselves from them as a noble Germanic race which must keep its blood pure and unmixed? (page 21).

"Every attempt to stigmatize the Jews because of their racial composition or origin has failed utterly. The Jews are the related strains of races . . . which created the ancient Semitic culture at a time that northern Europe was in chaos and ignorance, (page 23)

"We do not concede that religious difference has had any disadvantageous or disturbing effect on our attitude toward our Jewish neighbors. True religion does not separate; it always binds. Harshness, unkindness and contempt should never be directed against one's fellow beings under the subterfuge of religion, (page 48)

"Today it seems like sheer madness that in the Middle Ages Jews were accused of maliciously poisoning the wells in order to spread the plague. There will be a day in Germany when it will be remembered with the deepest shame that the Jews were accused of forcing us into the World War and that this accusation fell on believing ears. As long as the outcome of the war looked favorable, the Pan-Germans celebrated it as their war. Once Germany's power and glory was destroyed, the same nationalists tried to cast all blame from themselves onto the Jews, knowing how easy it was to instigate the masses to anti-Semitism. The Jew again had to serve as a scape-goat, (page 209)

"Shouldn't all who claim to be good Christians, who are followers of Him who gave humanity the Golden Rule, admit that hatred for Jewry, that is, for a people, whose names were borne by the founders of Christianity, is a sin against God and His Commandments? The Jews are neither enemies of our people nor of our religion and church. They have worked together, fought together and bled together with us for Germany 's greatness, salvation and future; they have a belief different from ours, but our belief has its origin in theirs as the bud and the fruit has its origin in the seed. When the forefathers of the present blonde 'noble men or of the pious German Christians had scarcely climbed the first steps of civilization, the Israelites had created a religious lore and a cultural monument which formed the principles of all finer spiritual belief in God and all higher morality, (page 214)

"Our Jewish citizens have an honest right to place their abilities and talents into fair competition with their Christian brethren for the good of the community. Don't we make this more difficult for them by deprecating them, by being hateful and by falsely accusing them? Whoever gathers the essence of Judaism from history stands with awe before the spirit of this great cultural and religious phenomenon." (page 230)

In "The Mission of Moses" (Prosaic Writings, 2nd period), the great national poet, Friedrich Schiller, says of Jewry: "The founding of the Jewish state by Moses is one of the most important accomplishments that has taken place in history—important for its effect on the world, this effect enduring to the very moment. Two religions that rule the greater portion of the inhabited earth—Christianity and Mohammedanism—look down on the religion of the Hebrews and yet without this religion, they never would have existed . . .

"Yes, in a certain sense it is undeniably true that we owe a great deal of the enlightenment that we enjoy today to the Mosaic faith. For through it a valuable truth, which long neglected reason might have found only after a long development, the doctrine of one God, was spread provisionally only among the people and was retained by them as an object of blind faith until the enlightened minds among them could attain a concept of reason.

"In this way a great portion of humanity was spared the sad errors to which polytheism would inevitably lead. And the Hebrew position has this exceptional advantage—the religion of the wise men was not directly opposed to the religion of the people, which was the case among the enlightened pagans. From the standpoint of their religion, the Hebrews must be regarded as an important universal, historical people; everything bad that has been said about this people, all the efforts of witless minds to deprecate their qualities will not hinder us from being fair to them!"

The Nazis know that Goethe's words are sacred relics to

many Germans. Therefore, they give Goethe the stage once in a while. But how? They quote the following passage from Goethe's humorous poem "Das Jahrmarktfest zu Plundersweilern" (The Annual Fair at Plundersweilern):

"The Jew loves money and fears danger. He knows how to carry money out of the country with very little effort and without much risk through commerce and tribute." The anti-Semite who cites this passage does not mention that Goethe placed these words in the mouth of Haman, an enemy to the Jews and that they are immediately followed by the King's words— "I know only too well, my friend, I am not blind. That is done by others who are not circumcised."

A person so free of prejudices as Goethe knew only too well that attributes and faults were the possession of Jews as of all peoples. He told Banker Lemmel of Prague that not only did he not hate Jews but felt a respect and an admiration for these creators of the Bible who had produced so many talented and sensitive men. In Wilhelm Meister's "Wanderjahren", Goethe praises the self-sufficiency, bravery, soundness and tenacity of the Jews. Goethe was on the friendliest terms with the philosopher, Herz, the musician, Meyerbeer, the Berlin art collector, Friedlander and the Prague banker, Lemmel. He had a close friendship with Marianne Meyer, later Marianne von Eybenberg, and her sister Sarah. The deep passionate feeling he had for Rachel Lewin, later Rachel Varnhagen, was an inspiration to him and his work. Goethe had befriended the painter, Oppenheimer, and the poet, Michael Beer, without ever considering them as Jews. They were simply his friends, irrespective of creed.

A recent investigator, Raimund Eberhard, has published some material on Goethe's interest in the Old Testament. Goethe embodied his knowledge of Hebrew and the Old Testament in his "Israel in der Wäste" (Israel in the Desert). The Prologue to Goethe's "Faust" was written according to the introduction to the Book of Job.

CHAPTER 5

Lies About Jewish Usury

The Nazis have decried to the world that the racial characteristics of the Jew predispose him to usury. They claim that the Jew has a usurer's soul. Only the stupid and the misinformed could believe such rubbish. An analysis of the occupations of the Jews before and after the diaspora will prove the falsity of this claim.

The ancient Jews were a landed people. They were mostly farmers and had little to do with commerce. According to the Torah, the promised blessing of the faithful lay in the prospering of the fruits of the field. Gideon was threshing wheat when called to command the army. Boaz, David's great-grandfather, was a farmer. The Prophet Elijah received the divine call when he was plowing his land with 12 span of oxen. Most of the Jewish scholars were craftsmen. When the famous Rabbi Gamliel came to appease his opponent, Joshua, he found him busy fashioning needles.

Cardinal Innitzer of Vienna wrote the following article entitled "Social Conditions in Palestine at the Time of Jesus," in 'The Friend of the Workers," a brochure published in 1932.

"At the time of Jesus Christ, the Jews were essentially an agricultural people. Farming was the main occupation of the Jews of Galilee, a province, which, as the Jewish historian Flavius Josephus reported, was entirely cultivated, and looked like a huge garden. The wheat of Galilee, of Chorazin and of Kfar Nahum, brought high prices. The Jewish peasant harvested five times the amount of seed planted on his acres but in years of abundance, he harvested as much as one hundred times the amount. (Matthew 13:8) In droughtless years grain was even exported. Besides wheat, barley, oats, rye, millet and rice, the Jews cultivated various vegetables and legumes. Palestine was rich in grapes, figs, olives, pomegranates, carob-beans, plums, almonds, dates, apples, pears, peaches and apricots. Because of the profusion of wine and oil in Palestine, both of these products could be exported. Wine and honey were made from Palestinian dates. Pliny praised Judea for its dates, as he praised Egypt for its spices.

"In addition to crops, the Jews also raised cattle. The city of Jerusalem required many sheep, oxen and goats for its inhabitants and for the daily sacrifices in the Temple. Squabs, chickens, geese and ducks were also brought to market in Jerusalem. Fisheries flourished along the shores of the Lake of Genezareth and the Mediterranean Sea. When Jesus first made his appearance, Tiberius was the center of the fishing industry. Several of the Apostles were fishermen. In Jerusalem the fishermen had their own Fish-Gate close to the Temple.

"Salt, asphalt, phosphorus and pitch were found in the Dead Sea. The famous asphalt of Palestine is known today as Jewish-pitch or Jewish-resin. Iron mines prospered in Lebanon and in Idumea. A fine scent was distilled from the roses and henna was made from the cypress flowers. According to Jewish literary sources, there were more than forty different types of handicrafts at the time of Jesus. The Talmud states that every father must teach his son a craft. Even those learned in the Scrolls, and even the High Priests had to learn some manual art. Jesus was a craftsman; he is mentioned in the Gospels as a carpenter, the son of a carpenter. The Gospels also tell us that the craft passed on from father to son. Some families had brought their craft to such an art that they carefully concealed the secret of their technique. Many cities were famous for articles they manufactured; Sepphoris was renowned for its fabrics, Beth-Shean for its linens, Bethsaida for its fish and Ligdal Zabbaim for its dyes. At the time of Jesus, some Jews were weavers of byssus and others, potters. (1-Chronicles 4:21-23). The Talmud refers occasionally to dye and ceramics workshops.

"The Gospels, however, seldom refer to crafts but rather to farming as the every day work of the Jews. Perhaps more did not develop among them because they could not compete with the cheaper foreign products sold in Palestine. The non-Hebrew, alien names for such common articles as towels, sandals, felt hats and chairs would indicate that this was the case. The small farmer mentioned in the Gospels and in the Mishnah dwelt in the villages and in small country towns. Aided by his wife and children, he tilled the soil and struggled for a livelihood. Most of what he harvested he needed for himself and his family. He would sell his surplus in the city in order to buy necessary articles for the house. This small farmer could scarcely save anything. Drought, crop-failure or sickness became a catastrophe. The farmer had to contract debts, became a wage-earner and soon entered the vassalage of a landed proprietor. Several of his sons were obliged to become day laborers and wage-earners because according to the Jewish laws of heredity, the first born received a double inheritance. Thus there was very little left for the remaining children. They could no longer live on the soil; they were proletarians oppressed by need, whose only possession was physical energy. If they found no work, they deteriorated into a sort of rag proletariat. In his Sermon on the Mount, Jesus praised these poor and oppressed listeners for patiently bearing their poverty and for making a virtue of their indigence. It is they who could not fulfill the numerous precepts of the Jewish law because of their economic circumstances, and their co-religionists cursed them for their ignorance. (John 7:49.)

"There were also some farmers who managed to save enough to conduct other businesses on the side. They formed the Jewish business element. There were comparatively few landed proprietors. They were essentially members of royal or ecclesiastical families. We meet such characters in the parable of the dishonest steward (Luke 16:1-8) and in the parable of the wicked husbandmen. (Matthew 21:28) Joseph of Aramathaea (Mark 15:43), the honorable counsellor may have belonged to this class. The expression 'honorable' used by Mark in his Gospel seems to designate a landed proprietor. Joseph actually was a rich man and possessed a garden with a rock sepulchre in Jerusalem. The Counsellor Nicodemus (John 3:1; 7:50; 19:39) appeared to be opulent, for he brought a rich bounty of ointments to the burial of Jesus.

Rabbinical lore mentions the wheat, oil, wine and wood dealers in Jerusalem. During the siege of the Romans in the winter of 69-70, the peasants set fire to the well-stocked granaries of Nogdimon Ben Gorjon, a grain merchant.

"Besides the full-fledged farmers, there were also a few tenant farmers who cultivated the soil and in return received a corresponding portion of the produce (25-50%). The parable of the rebellious vintagers (Matthew 2:3 3-43) indicates that their relation with the landed proprietors was not a friendly one. In addition to tenants there were contractors and lessees who worked the estates for a certain percentage of the crop or for a sum deducted from the rental.

"In the Gospels and letters of the Apostles, occasional mention is made of day laborers and workers. The Palestinian laborers, called Likutoth, hired out for no longer than six years but no less than one day. They were usually impoverished vintners or their sons who had to work for the wealthy farmers, often for the balance of their lives. The workers, on the other hand, hired out only for specific trades. In the Talmud, mention is also made of the unemployed, and in the parable of the workers in the vineyard (Matthew 20:1-16) the lord of the manor who goes to the market to employ workers, finds them idly standing about in the square because no one had put them to work. The employers generally struck an oral agreement with the workers. Some times a written contract was drawn up, and there was a fine in the event of breach of contract. In general the Jewish worker was better situated than the worker in other countries, because the essentials of life in Palestine were simpler, and the number of rich men was smaller than elsewhere. Besides farmlands, there were industrial workers. Their work lasted ten hours a day, and for this they received one drachma or one dinar = 1½ shilling. Last to be mentioned are the menials and domestics whose only possession was the energy by which they lived." Thus does Cardinal Innitzer describe conditions in Palestine at the time of Jesus.

The tribal migrations brought many Jews to Germany. Under Charles the Great the Jews ceased settling in Germany in large numbers. From then on few immigrations took place. The Jews were treated as Romans by the Franks and the Burgundians, who allowed them to engage in agriculture, trade and commerce without any restrictions. They travelled down rivers and over seas on their own ships. They practiced medicine, and Jewish physicians were consulted by Church dignitaries. The Jews knew how to handle weapons and took an active part in the conflicts between Clodowig and Theoderic during the siege of Aries. The commerce that the Jews advanced during the early Middle Ages was a blessing to the peoples among whom they lived. The Jews did not enter commerce as an evasion of manual labor, for commercial enterprise entailed great danger and many difficulties in those days. Commerce meant travel, and merchants on business trips always were beset upon by bands of robbers. Robber knights lurked behind shrubbery, fell on unsuspecting merchants and seized their goods. It was no easy matter to defend oneself against such perils. It required much courage and quick thinking. The Jews at that time were more cultured and capable than the Germans. They had at their command a number of languages, had friends and relatives everywhere and possessed a common language in Hebrew. They were indeed the most appropriate group to handle commerce. This was not overlooked by Charlemagne (768-814). who appreciated the importance of commerce to the new empire he had founded. He realized that the Jews, by virtue of their commercial talent, would be of welfare to the people and would raise their standard of living.

Later religious differences gradually became emphasized, and fanaticism led to many violent deeds, before which humanity stands shamefaced.

In 545 the 4th Council of Orleans enacted severe measures against the Jews. The Council of Macon in 581 attempted to reduce the Jews to a lower position in society; the Jews were forbidden to act as judges or as tax-collectors in order that "the Christian population would not seem to be subject to them." In Spain, King Reccared, prohibited Jews from marrying Christians, from acquiring Christian slaves and from occupying public office.

Despite these measures the Jews were not disturbed in Germany before the Crusades. They were allowed to own land and suffered little hatred or contempt. When in 1084, Bishop Ruediger Huozmann of Speyer converted the hamlet of Alt-Speier into a town, he felt that the appearance of the city could be improved in no better way than to grant living quarters and privileges to the Jews. Besides freedom of commerce, the Jews in Neu-Speyer were allowed to own farms and vineyards and hire Christians as aids and servants. To protect them from the molestations of the mob, Ruediger gave the Jews their own section of the city which they were asked to fortify and defend.

During the Crusades and in the period thereafter, Jews could not participate in agriculture, trade and commerce. They were only allowed to sell old clothes and practice usury.

This was a dreadful blow to the Jew. He was actually forced into usury. The lending of money at interest is not sanctioned by the Jewish religion. The Torah does not grant the Jews the right to practice usury. In fact, verses 19 and 20 of the 23rd chapter of the book of Moses forbid the taking of interest. Such chapters of the Old Testament as Ezekiel, 19 verses 8 and 9 and Psalms 15:5, praise those who demand no interest. The Rabbis recommended that money be lent without interest even to idol-worshippers. In the Talmud, the Shulchan Aruch Choschen Mishpat, 34-29, states that "if an usurer desires to acquire the right to bear witness he must tear up all promissory notes, close up his evil trade and never take interest, even from a non-Jew, whether or not his needs require that he take it. In the history of the Jews before Christ as well as in the early history of the Diaspora, there is not a single case of Jewish usury. Neither Roman nor Greek writers who ridiculed the Jews ever mention a Jewish usurer. Jerusalem fell and later the Roman empire fell; the Jews were scattered throughout the world, and a thousand years went by during which no mention was made of Jewish usury. Even the Church Fathers who were greatly concerned about the Jews and wrote very unfavorably about them did not report usury among the Jews. Not even the "Catechism of the anti-Semites", which includes every unpleasant reference to Jews, can cite the case of a single Jewish usurer before the 12th century.

In the later Middle Ages the Jews were barred from all offices and honors, guilds and corporations, trade and commerce. Thus the majority ofJews were damned to usury or starvation. Only a small number could devote themselves to the limited occupations open to them, such as money-changing, banking and trading in precious stones.

The great landowners were the ultimate gainers of the Jewish usurer. The odium of usury they left to the Jews. The fruits of usury they placed in their own pockets. (Coudenhove-Kalergi, "Essence of Anti-Semitism"). A church law, based on the previously mentioned passage from The Old Testament, forbade lending money at interest. In order not to violate this law, good "Christians" made the Jews practice usury so that once the latter acquired a fortune, they were soon deprived of it on grounds of illegal acquisition. The Jews never saw the money again. It disappeared in the pockets of their "protectors".

When Hitler states that the lending of money at interest was introduced to the western world by Jewry, he defies historical facts. He obviously has not heard how the plebeians fled to the Holy Mountain in Rome to avoid the unrestricted usury of the Aryan patricians, and how this exodus led to the legal setting of a maximal interest. Thus 560 ***years before the destruction ofJerusalem, when there was not a single Jew*** in ***all of "Aryan Rome ", let alone a Jewish moneylender, the city was plagued by usury.***

Resolutions of Church councils during the early and later Middle Ages indicate that Christians, even ecclesiastics, carried on money businesses despite the church law against the taking of interest. That these Christian money businesses in the Middle Ages often assumed the character of oppressing usury is illustrated by the interesting fact that in 1430 the Florentines asked the Jews to help them fight exorbitant rates of interest, prevalent at the time, which they were unable to meet. It is, therefore, apparent that the Jews did not bring usury to the Occident but found it there and that during the Middle Ages, Christians also carried on usury, frequently in a more oppressing fashion than the Jews. It has been established that the Jews did not enter into money businesses in antiquity and in the Middle Ages but were forced to enter them.

When the Jews were dispersed among the peoples, the Talmud forbade them to lend money at interest to non-Jews, but in exceptional cases permitted a rate of interest consistent with the lender's expenses and not for an increase in his personal fortune. (Baba Mezi'a, 70). The Jewish scholar, Maimonides, considered this interest-regulation binding. The ban on interest was never raised, but it was impossible for the Jews to observe it since every branch of industry was closed to them. Thus the Jews did not enter voluntarily into this disgraceful profession, contradictory to the laws of their religion. In his annotations to the aforementioned passage from the Talmud, Rabbi Jacob Tam, born in 1171, bitterly remarks that the law governing interest-taking from non-Jews cannot be observed. "They have not left us a single branch of industry by which we can maintain ourselves and meet the high taxes that our landlords impose upon us."

That is the story of Jewish usury. I do not deny that there are still Jews who practice usury of their own volition. But I take exception to Hitler's remark that all Jews are usurers. If the battle against usury is to be morally justified, it must be waged against all usurers.

Until the end of the last century there were no Jews in Norway. Previous to this time the population had been so badly exploited by usurers that the laws of 1842 regulating the limitation of interest had to be revised and restated in 1851. In t**he year** 1845, ***when there were no Jewish money lenders in England, debtors had to pay from twenty to sixty per cent interest.***

A band of usurers recently worked the environs of Vienna. They took as high as 80% annual interest from the poor farmers. Not a single Jew was found among these exploiters.

Gentile usurers are seldom mentioned by the newspapers out of respect to their adherence to the Christian faith. When these usurers are condemned and sentenced before the court, a small notice appears in the newspaper, and the matter is settled.

In the case of court proceedings against a Jewish usurer, the crime, as such, is scarcely mentioned while that of being a Jew is greatly emphasized. Names of Jewish usurers have been revived a dozen times, sometimes by direct reference, other times by obvious allusion. Frequently cases are fabricated, and we read of "A Jew In Floridsdorf" or "A Jewish Cut-Throat." The result: every Jew is thought to be a usurer. I defy the anti-Semites to prove that more than one per cent of usurers all over the world are Jews.

The Jews did not discover usury. They were driven to it against their will from the Middle Ages to the beginning of the last century. Today no more Jews than non-Jews engage in money-lending. If the remaining Jewish usurers were to be removed, usury would still run rampant as long as people are oppressed by need.

CHAPTER 6

Lies About the Talmud

The Talmud has suffered much libel in the past. It is still libeled today. Suspicion has been aroused that there are passages in the Talmud that urge the Jews to take undue advantage of non-Jews. There are no such passages. The Talmud enjoins the Jews to be honorable in their dealings with one another and with Gentiles.

The purpose and goal of the Talmudic legal code is to fulfill social needs and religious truths. The precepts and ceremonies, laws and benedictions in the Talmud are fundamentally opposed to evil and dedicated to the welfare of humanity. The Talmud is a continuation of the Biblical law. Like the Bible, it is devoted to the interests of society. It is concerned with administering to the needy and the sick, with aiding widows, orphans and prisoners and with protecting the working classes from exploitation. The Talmud stands for faith, charity and justice.

The Nazis attempt to justify their vicious anti-Semitic policy by "quoting" from the Talmud. These quotations amount to sheer distortions of the original. So that my readers may realize the falsity of these passages, I am going to discuss the factual material in the Talmud.

The Nazis claim that the Talmud encourages the Jews to exploit the Gentiles, men, women and children. The Talmudic laws decree, however, that in business and in the practice of charity a non-Jew must be treated in the same manner as a Jew. The Talmudists have even written that Jews should visit the sick among the idol-worshippers, bury their dead and feed their poor. In Psalms 145, 9 we find: "The Lord is good to all: and his tender mercies are over all his works."

The Nazis contend that the Talmud "commends the spoliation of Gentiles through usury ". That is a malicious lie! The Bible expressly forbids the Jews to lend at interest. Other peoples who loaned money to Jews demanded interest; hence the Jews required interest on loans to their nieghbors. That was merely a measure of reciprocity. Nevertheless, the Jewish scholars expressly forbade their coreligionists to exact interest from non-Jews. (Talmud, Baba Mezi'a 71a) Exploitation of Jews or non-Jews was never condoned. The Jewish masses held usury in contempt.

The Talmud decrees that "It is forbidden to rob a Jew or a non-Jew of an object of the slightest value or to hold back what has been taken." (Choschem Hamishpat: 3 59,1) "He who steals an object of the value of a peruta violates the commandment 'Thou shalt not steal', and must make amends whether the victim be Jew or non-Jew." (C. H. 348,2) "He who measures or weighs falsely for Jew or idol-worshipper violates the injunction: Thou shalt not be dishonest in measuring and in weighing dry and liquid stock'. (C. H. 231,1)

"It is forbidden to cheat people in business or to steal their mind (let them believe that you wish to do them a favor). If there is a defect in the goods, the purchaser must be informed. No nebela meat (meat not slaughtered according to ritual) may be sold even to a non-Jew if he assumes that it has been appropriately slaughtered." (C. H. 228,6)

This ought to be sufficient evidence to disprove the malicious slander of the Nazis that the Talmud permits Jews to exploit and oppress non-Jews. The Nazis are wont to cite passages from Sanhedrin, 37a, and Baba Mezi'a 3 b. In all of Sanhedrin, 37a there is no reference whatsoever to non-Jews, while such a passage as Baba Mezi'a 3 b does not exist.

Years ago a case involving a certain Professor Rohling and Rabbi Bloch came up before the Supreme Court in Vienna. Two Christian professors, August Wünsche and Theodor Nöldecke, testified before the court as authorities on the Talmud. These scholars declared that the accusations levelled against the Talmud were completely false and without any foundation. Prominent anti-Semites who spread their calumnies among the Christian people of Germany are acquainted undoubtedly with the book of Dr. Joseph Kopp, a Christian attorney who defended Rabbi Bloch, entitled "Zur Judenfrage nach den Akten des Processes Rohling-Bloch", 1866. (On the Jewish Question According to the Data of the Rohling-Bloch Case.) Although this book clearly exposes the fraudulent claim of the Anti-Semites, the latter prefer to blind themselves to the truth and refuse to acknowledge the real facts of a suit that lasted years. The experts in this trial further testified that the Talmud is nothing other than a compilation of oral tradition and debates held in the temples of learning from the time of Moses to the 5th Century A. D. The brief but literally reproduced debates of the schools of Palestine and of Babylonia comprise the essence of the Talmud. There is a voluminous Babylonian Talmud and a small Palestinian Talmud. The Talmud is not the work of one man but the product of many centuries of spiritual observation and gives an accurate picture of the historical development of the Jews.

The Talmud in content is as colorful and variegated as life itself. There is nothing in heaven or on earth within the vision and experience of the people of that era that has not been discussed in the Talmud.

The Talmud today has validity only insofar as rite and religion are concerned. Its civil, penal and administrative regulations are no longer followed. According to the Jewish precepts, the laws of the State are the laws to be observed. The Jews assert their rights according to the laws of the country in which they live. When one Jew sues another Jew, he does not appeal to the Talmud but to the laws of the State.

Of approximately 16 million Jews in the world, a minority are truly familiar with the Talmud. The Jews of Western and Eastern Europe who have not studied the Talmud in childhood or in later life know of it only by reference. Yet the anti-

Semites have the unmitigated gall to distort Talmudic passages and then tell the public that all Jews are bound by such Talmudic "laws", in the hope of discrediting them and arousing antipathy toward them. The Talmud is no mystery. The Nazis have had sufficient opportunity to inform themselves of the truth.

Many commentaries on the Talmud have been written by both Christians and Jews. Such outstanding scholars as Franz; Delitzsch and Fiebig have made a scientific study of the Talmud. It has been translated into all the major languages of Europe. There are, to be sure, fraudulent translations of the Talmud, such as that of a certain Justus, alias Aron Briman. Justus was first baptized a Protestant and later a Catholic. In 1865 he met his fate in Vienna where he was condemned to imprisonment and exile on grounds of forgery. Professor Delitzsch of Leipzig called this man's "translation" of the Talmud "a pack of infernal lies!"

Dr. Noldecke considered Rohling's translation of the Talmud a brazen audacity. Professor Herman Strack regarded it as "a rare combination of ignorance, hatred and malice." He stated also that it was copied from another false translation. A certain Dr. Ecker of Münster, in turn, published Justus-falsification as his own work. Dr. Bickel, a professor of Catholic Theology, called this edition of it "a fraud perpetrated by learned swindlers." Delitzsch angrily said of such forgers: "The God of Truth still lives and so does the risen Christ, who will show the disgracers of His name how to honor Him . . . The Rohlings and the Justuses who serve Him with lies, will be struck dead by these very lies!"

I shall quote several doctrinary sentences from the Torah, the Talmud and the later scriptures to prove that the religious precepts of the Jews are of universal moral value. The best known of the Jewish major ethical laws are the Ten Commandments. Every point that is not covered in the Commandments may be found in the Jewish scriptures. Here respect for the property of others is greatly emphasized. In the "Ethics of the Fathers," 11,12, we find that "The property of others should be dearer to thee than thine own." "Any violation of the property of others is not only a sin against man but against God."

"He who takes the property of another is doomed to drought." (Tanit, 7b)

"It is worse to rob a person than to steal holy property". (Baba Batra, 88b)

"He whose hands are stained with stolen goods is not heard by the Lord when he calls to Him". (Shamat Rabba, 0.22)

The following legend from the Babylonian Talmud illustrates how misuse of another's property was synonymous with theft. "A silver vessel was once stolen from pious Mar Sutra in an inn. When he saw a man wash his hands and dry them on the towel of another man he said to himself: 'He who appropriates the things of another might well be a thief.' When he accused him, the culprit actually confessed his guilt." (Baba Mezi'a, 24a)

"Not even an honest person should be given the opportunity to steal . . ." (Tanchum, paragraph Vayishlach)

"It is a graver offense to rob the dead than the living; for he who robs the living can return the property and ask the victim for forgiveness, but he who robs the dead never can return the property and cannot ask for forgiveness." (Ebel Rabbati, c.9)

According to the Talmudic law it is forbidden to enter the home of another without permission, even to demand the return of one's own property. "Thou shalt not enter the home of thy neighbor to fetch thy property without his knowledge, for this also is akin to thievery." (Baba Kamma, 27b)

In his great codification of the Jewish Law, Maimonides (11254204) devoted much of his efforts to those chapters on robbery and theft. (Hilchot Gesela and Hilchot Ganeyvah) The Hilkot De'ot, which corresponds in portion to the "Ethics of the Fathers", states that: "Thou shouldst always speak well of they neighbor and protect his property as thou protecteth thine own property."

"Just as the creditor is forbidden to exact payment when he knows that it is impossible for the debtor to pay him, so is the debtor forbidden to withhold money from the creditor and to say to him 'Go and come again.' (Ethics 328.) It is just as faithless and disloyal to make a loan and squander and spend it heedlessly so that the creditor finds nothing when he asks for payment. Who acts thusly is wicked even if the creditor is well-to-do, "The wicked borroweth and payeth not; but the righteous dealth graciously and giveth." (Psalms 3,7:21.)

"It is forbidden to buy stolen goods from a thief, indeed it is a cardinal sin, for in this way a thief is abetted and permitted to commit other thefts. Were he to find no one to buy his stolen goods, he would not steal." (Mishnah-Torah, Hilkot Ganey vah,V)

According to the Talmudic law, every business that offends moral customs is illegal and, as such, subject to closure at any time. Even if purchaser and seller agree between themselves that no objections to over-charging will be raised, the law against exhorbitant profits still remains valid. No dishonest means may be applied in any business to give the purchaser a false conception of the value and price of the wares. If these wares contain any defects or blemishes, the purchaser must be informed of them. A general statement which evasively implies that purchased goods are not free from blemishes is not satisfactory. The same holds for the price. Exorbitant profits are prohibited particularly in the matter of essential commodities. If in a transaction the purchaser has been charged the full price plus a sixth of the value of the goods, the purchase can be returned, unless, at the close of the deal, the purchaser is expressly informed that he has paid more than the customary price in the locality. Price-raisers and cheaters were punished as unscrupulous people who seriously threatened the welfare of the State and Society. (Baba Batra, 90b)

The Talmud always places great emphasis on honesty.

"When man is brought to reckoning, he will be asked 'have you been honest in commerce and trade? " (Sabbar, 3 I a)

"Great is honesty, for who practices his profession honestly, at the same time fulfills all commands of the Torah". (Midrash Godol; Godoloh 12, Beth Hamidrash) -

"He who does not keep his word is like an idol-worshipper." (Sanhedrin, 92a)

"Who has punished the generation of the flood and of the Tower of Babel and of the Sodomites because of their sins will also seek him out who has not kept his word of honor." (Baba Mezi'a, 48a)

It was said of Rabbi Saffra that: "the truth speaks in his heart". (Psalm 15,2) Rabbi Saffra once wanted to sell something. While he was reading his Sh'ma, a man came to him and offered him a price for the article. Since the Rabbi could not interrupt his reading to answer him, the man thought that he had offered him too small a price and thereupon increased it. After he had finished his prayers, the Rabbi said: "Take the object for the price offered me at first, for I originally had intended to give it to thee at that price." (Makkot, 24a)

"One should not promise to give a child something and then not give it to him, because in this way he will learn to lie." (Baba Mezi'a, 49a)

Exhortations to honesty were made by later authorities.

Saadya Gaon (92-942) states in his Emunot V'deyot, (Doctrines of Revelation and Reason): "cheat not deliberately in thy dealings with others, non-Jews or Jews. Be not impatient with those of thy faith; deal honestly in thy business, tell no one that he may purchase goods for this or that price when that is not the case; pretend not that thou wishest to buy when it is not thy intention to buy. Such deeds are unworthy of an Israelite." (Book of the Pious): ***Zunz,*** "Geschichte und Literatur", pages 135 and 136.

"If thou canst nourish thyself with the little thou possesseth, take not from others to increase thy wealth for those who take from others have no happiness."

"There is no blessing on the money of those who grasp their money tightly, who practice usury, who deal in false weights and measures and who are not honest in trade." ***(Zunz,*** page 137)

"When one refuses public aid because of an exaggerated sense of shame, he may perpetrate an injustice on a third person. Thus, one who lives in a dwelling that he rents and is not in a position to pay the rent that is due, refuses the aid offered him with the remark that he never accepts charity and thereby acts injustly toward the owner of the house, who is not responsible for his support. Therefore, it is fitting that he accept this in order to pay his debt." (Book of the Pious, 867; Zunz, 1046)

"A forgetful man should not be supervisor of the poor. He also should not become the custodian of the property of others, for detriment to this property might well arise from forgetfulness." (Book of the Pious, 907; ***Zunz,*** 329)

"Whoever falsely measures or weighs in trading with Jews or non-Jews, violates a command of the Torah. It is strictly forbidden to overcharge a non-Jew; rather should one be most accurate with him. Neither movable nor immovable property must be sold without informing the purchaser if there is a suit pending concerning said goods, for even if the seller is responsible for damages to the purchaser, no one should give out money for anything that brings him into controversy." (Mishnah-Torah, Hilchot Mechira XIX.)

'Thou shalt not mix water with wine. If a dealer finds water in wine he can sell it only on the condition that he informs the purchaser about it; the latter cannot sell the wine in turn to another purchaser, for in this way he might cheat the purchaser." (Daas, 18-6)

"Anything that is known to be stolen or goods that might well be stolen must not be purchased. In this way wool, milk or young lambs must not be purchased from shepherds." (Mishnah-Torah, Hilchot 6-1)

"One must not accept favors from people who are known to be robbers, who ply dishonest trades or who are suspected of not being in righteous possession of their goods." (Daas 5-9; Mishnah-Torah, Baba Kamma 10-9)

"Only those articles may be purchased from women, domestics and children that appear to belong to them rightfully."

(Mishnah-Torah, Hilchot Ganeyvoh; Mishnah-Torah, Baba Kamma 9)

"Neither wood nor fruit may be purchased from gardeners. If the purchase takes place on the open market where the gardeners display baskets and wagons, one may purchase from them." (Baba Kamma, VI, 3)

"The tailor who has received material and trimmings for work is obliged to return to the owner all scraps, even it they are no wider than three fingers, and thread, even if it scarcely can be pulled through the needle." "Likewise the carpenter is obliged to return to the owner all chips and scraps of material. In general, the custom of the country is binding in such matters." (Daas, 7-8, Baba Kamma 118b)

Avoid anything that resembles thievery and cheating. Bet not with thy neighbor lor anything of value; let not thy money out on interest unbeknown to thy neighbor, nor lend it to him on interest. "Thou shalt not play with dice." (Moses Cohen ben Eliezer; The Small Book of the Pious, lib)

"Thou shalt not cheat thine own nor the Gentile, even in words." (Eliezer Asharti Sepher Haradim; Book of the God-fearing, 5c)

Menassah ben Israel (1604-57) in his "Salvation of the Jews", translated by Marcus Hertz; and published in Mendelsohn's "Collective Works", states on page 247 that:

"The teachers of the Talmud hold that restitution is a deed

deserving of the praise of God and of the Holy Writ. When the honest and wise Rabbi Simon ben Chettach bought a mule from a pagan, he found a jewel of great value under the mule's halter. The Rabbi voluntarily returned the jewel to its owner who was not aware of the jewel's existence. The honest Rabbi declared that he had bought the mule but not the jewel. In this way God and his Jewish Nation were honored."

"Be honest in thy trade for the first question that God will direct to thy soul when it appeareth before his throne is: 'Hast thou always been honest in thy dealing with others?' If a debt is due thee, force not payment of it neither from Jews nor from non-Jews . . . Take care not to seize the property of others.

Take care not to steal the thoughts of others, that is, deceive not another as to thy intentions, even if he belongeth to another faith." (Sabar, 31 a)

Whoever reads these Talmudic laws and still maintains that the Talmud is an immoral work and that it encourages the Jews to exploit the Christians can be nothing else but a scoundrel or a fool.

CHAPTER 7

The Ritual Murder Lies

The Jews were first accused of ritual murder in the 12th Century. From then on it was rumored that during the Easter season the Jews murdered Christian children and used their blood in the Passover rites. Confessions were extracted from the accused on the rack and by other means of torture, but they never amounted to genuine evidence. Neither then nor in the following centuries could a perpetrator of ritual murder ever be found.

A little thought on the subject will reveal the history of ritual murder trials as a tragic stupidity. If there had been any foundation for this accusation more than six or seven such trials would have taken place over a period of 2,000 years.

The Jewish scriptures make no mention of ritual murder. Anyone acquainted with them will confirm this fact. Confirmation has been rendered by such outstanding scholars as Delitzsch and Nöldecke. The anti-Semites, however, claim that it is the secret documents of the Jews that foster the blood rite. The Jews possess no secret documents. If such documents existed, the anti-Semites would have discovered them long ago. Chapter 17 of the third book of Moses, and other passages in the Holy Scriptures strictly forbid the use of blood. So great is the aversion to blood among the Jews that the Kosher meat process requires repeated rinsing and washing to remove all traces of blood. Yet rumors of blood ritual are constantly revived.

Toward the latter half of the nineteenth century a certain Dr. Rohling, whose name (German: "barbarian") was indicative of his character and who was very influential at the Austrian court in his capacity of canon and professor of theology, swore that the Jews practiced ritual murder and that they were encouraged in this practice by certain passages in the Scriptures prescribing the use of Christian blood for ritual purposes. This remark aroused great indignation. Dr. Jacob Bloch, a Rabbi, made vehement public declaration in a Viennese newspaper that if Rohling took such an oath, it amounted to perjury. He challenged him to prove his statement before a court of law. In the subsequent trial Delitzsch and Nöldecke testified that the passages cited by Rohling were gross falsifications. Rohling began to feel uncomfortable. The trial lasted two years. Twelve days before it terminated, he recanted, retracted his statement and assumed all court costs. Rohling's career had come to an end. His writings were banned and placed on the Expurgatory Index of the Church, and Kaiser Franz; Joseph divested him of his offices. He died in exile in Salzburg.

In the dark past ritual murder accusations frequently have been levelled by many groups against their enemies.

According to Gibbons, the Romans accused the Early Christians of mutilating a new-born child completely dipped in flour and drinking its blood in their secret meetings. During the reign of Hadrian and under Marcus Aurelius and Lucius Verus, many Christians attempted to demonstrate to the Romans in oral and written manner, the invalidity of anti-Christian polemics. Among those who defended the honor of Christianity were Origenes, Eusebius, Justinus and Minicius, Felix and Athenagoras.

Athenagoras wrote: "According to our law, it is neither permissible to beat nor to blaspheme against those who curse us ... We also do not espouse the kind of justice that gives credence to like deserves like but strive to set an example to others by kindness and patience. Knowing that we follow such principles, who in his right mind could suspect us of being fiendish murderers? Furthermore even if we were to kill a human being, which is hardly possible, we would not eat his flesh ... If those who accuse us were asked whether they saw us commit the deed of which we are accused, I believe that not one of them would have the audacity to say that he had ..."

In a petition to Caesar Antonius, Justinus declared: "Ignorant people, driven by evil demons, spread this malicious rumor about . . . These evil persons, as tools of the devil have even dragged our men and women servants to the rack and by torturing them horribly, have forced them to confess crimes which the tormentors themselves have publicly committed . . ."

And Tertulian wrote:

"It has been said that we must kill and eat a child to perform our sacraments ... This will always be said as long as the rumor persists and as long as no investigations are made. The same thing is constantly repeated, and not once have you tried to investigate our crime . . ."

After Christianity rose to power, individual sects accused one another of mixing the blood of children with flour at Easter time and eating it. The Mohammedans also suspected the Christians of the same crime. The Chinese suspected the first Christian missionaries of many crimes, such as killing pregnant women and mutilating defenseless people. In 1870 the Spaniards accused the French Protestants and the Freemasons of having stolen and sacrificed a child who had been missing for a long time.

Thus it is essentially the same myth that one group tells about another.

A number of Papal Bulls denounced the ritual murder accusations against the Jews. In his Bull of July 5, 1247, Innocent IV declared to the Archbishops and Bishops of Germany:

"We have received a mournful complaint from the Jews of Germany, telling how some princes, both ecclesiastical and lay, together with other nobles and powerful persons in your cities and dioceses, devise evil plans against them and invent various pretexts in order to rob them unjustly of their goods, and gain possession thereof. This they do without stopping to consider prudently that it is from the archives of the Jews, so as to speak, that the testimonies of the Christian faith came forth. Holy Scripture pronounces among other injunctions of the Law "Thou shalt not kill", forbidding them when they celebrate the Passover even to touch any dead body. Nevertheless, they are falsely accused that, in that same solemnity, they make communion with the heart of a slain child. This is alleged to be enjoined by the Law, whereas in fact such an act is manifestly contrary to it. Moreover, if the body of a dead man is by chance found anywhere, they maliciously ascribe the cause of death to the action of the Jews.

"On this, and many other fictitious pretexts, they rage against the Jews and despoil them of their possessions, against God and Justice and the privileges mercifully granted to them by the Holy See; notwithstanding that they have never been convicted of them. By starvation, imprisonment and many heavy persecutions and oppressions they harass them, inflicting upon them diverse kinds of punishment, and condemning large numbers to a most shameful death. Hence the Jews, who are under the power of the aforesaid nobles, lords and princes, are in a worse condition than were their fathers in Egypt, and are compelled to go into exile from localities where they and their ancestors have dwelt from time immemorial. Wherefore, fearing that they would be utterly exterminated, they have thought well to have recourse to the wisdom of the Apostolic See. We, therefore, being unwilling that the aforesaid Jews should be unjustly harassed (seeing that the compassionate God expects their conversion, and that we believe, according to the testimony of the prophet, that the remnant of them shall be saved), do ordain that you show yourselves favourable and benign towards them. Duly redress all that has been wrought against the Jews in the aforesaid matter by the said prelates, nobles and potentates; and do not allow them in future to be unjustly molested by anybody on this or any other similar charge.

Given in Lyons on July 5th, in the fifth year of our Ponticate (1247)."

On September 25, 125 3, Innocent IV, was forced to issue another Bull against this spurious accusation. "Furthermore, we decree, in order to combat the corruption and avarice of evil people, that no one shall dare lay waste nor desecrate any Jewish cemetery nor exhume bodies with the pretense that he is looking for money, and that no one shall accuse them (the Jews) of using human blood in their religious rites, since in the Old Testament they are instructed not to use blood of any kind, let alone human blood. But since at Fulda and in several other places Jews were killed on the grounds of such a suspicion, we, by the authority of these presents, strictly forbid that this should be done in the future. If anyone dare to oppose this decree.... he shall be punished by the loss of his rank and office or be placed under a ban of excommunication."

On October 7, 1272, Gregory X issued a Bull stating:

"Furthermore, we decree that the testimony of Christians against Jews is valid only if it is combined with the testimony of a Jew, for Jews themselves cannot bear testimony against

Christians. It sometimes happens that certain Christians lose their children. The charge is then made against the Jews by their enemies that they have stolen and slain these children in secret, and have sacrificed the heart and blood. The fathers of the said children, or other Christians who are envious of the Jews, even hide their children in order to have a pretext to molest the Jews, and to extort money from them so as to pay their dues. They assert thereupon, most falsely, that the Jews have taken away these children and slain them, and have sacrificed the heart and blood. Yet their law expressly forbids the Jews to sacrifice or to eat or drink blood: even though it be of animals which have the hoof cloven. This has been confirmed in our curia on many occasions by Jews converted to the Christian faith. None the less, on this pretext many Jews have frequently been seized and detained, against all justice. We accordingly have determined that no Christian shall be allowed to make any allegations against the Jews on such a pretext. We command, moreover, that the Jews imprisoned on this account shall be released from prison, and that they shall not be arrested again on such groundless charge unless (which we think impossible) they are captured in flagrant crime."

On February 20, 1422 Pope Martin V issued a Bull denouncing the mistreatment of Jews on false indictments.

"To extort money from the Jews, to plunder and throw stones at their goods and possessions, sometimes Christians resort to pretexts and accusations and spread rumors in times of great mortality and other calamities that Jews throw poison in the wells and that they mix human blood with their unleavened bread. These crimes, of which they are so unjustly accused, are rumored about to contaminate people. The people are aroused by these accusations against the Jews, kill them, seek them out in their homes and torture them with relentless persecution and oppression. Considering that it behooves the Christian religion to offer the greatest protection to the Jews against their persecutors and oppressors, all the more expressly since they are held as witnesses of the true faith . . . We strictly forbid your corporate body (the clergy) ... to preach anything of or similar to this nature."

Pope Nicholas V gave out a similar Bull on November 5, 1447:

"We have heard with displeasure from the complaints of the Jews of Hungary, Poland, and Bohemia how for some years past, certain magistrates and their officials, bitter and mortal enemies of the Jews, blinded by hate and envy or as is more probable by cupidity, pretend, in order to despoil them of their goods, that the Jews kill little children and drink their blood." The Pope continues that this allegation was made in order to exacerbate the feeling of simple Christians against the Jews as a result of which the Jews were unjustly deprived, not only of their possessions, but in many cases of their lives.

Besides the Popes, many princes of the Church denounced ritual murder accusations. Cardinal Ganganelli made a report on this subject on December 4, 1759, the first part of which deals with the anti-Semitic prejudice of the population as the psychological basis for the blood accusation and the second portion with the falsity of evidence in ritual murder trials. Ganganelli's report and the verdict of the Inquisition Tribunal were further confirmed by Pope Clement XIII on January 10, 1760. The Pope then declared that there was no evidence of blood ritual among the Jews and hence, no basis for this accusation against them.

I should like to quote a statement made by the Archbishop of Volhynia in the Frankfurter Zeitung of May 25, 1913, regarding the Kiev blood trial:

"The people forget their Savior and in their hatred go so far as to accuse the Jews of such a heinous crime as ritual murder. Such ignorance is horrifying. They imagine that the Bible asks the Israelites to celebrate their Passover ceremony with blood. That is nothing but a myth, which is constantly revived. Those who believe that the Holy Scriptures command the Jews to spill blood have not read or do not understand them. I say that the rumor of a sect among the Jews using Christian blood is a damnable lie!"

So that my readers may realise how fraudulent is the claim of Jewish blood ritual, I should like to cite several instances culminating in trial.

In Frankfurt am Main in 1504 lived a Jew by the name of Gombchen, a butcher who possessed a considerable fortune. He also conducted a loan business on the side in keeping with the customs of the times. Among his customers in both businesses was Heinrich Bry, a shoemaker, always in debt and never able to meet his obligations. One day, for one reason or another, Bry killed his step-child and fled to Hanau where he later was apprehended. He subsequently confessed everything, adding that he had poured the murdered child's blood into a bowl and had brought it to Gombchen. The townspeople were greatly stirred by this turn of events, and everybody exclaimed that Bry was only a tool in the hands of a Jew. Gombchen was arrested and denied any guilt. Even after being tortured at the rack, he refused to confess what he had not committed. Meanwhile the case against Bry came up for trial. He was condemned to death and executed on November 4th, 1504. A few days before this date Bry admitted that he had falsely accused Gombchen and also repeated the same confession a few moments before the execution. Nevertheless Gombchen was held in custody for several weeks and was set free only after he had sworn an oath of truce, that is, promised not to seek revenge for the injustice he had suffered. Any impartial observer must admit that that medieval court of law, which would not have admitted a mistake very graciously, was completely convinced of the innocence of the defendant. And since that time not one trial over Jewish blood ritual has brought forth an iota of evidence to support the accusation.

The murder of Esther Solymossi on April I, 1882 in the Hungarian city of Tisza-Eszlar had great repercussions. Miss Solymossi, a servant girl had left her place of employment that day to do some shopping, and her way to market led past the Synagogue. On the same day, several local Jewish men, three Jews from other communities and the porter, Joseph Scharf, had met in the Synagogue to elect a Schochet. The anti-Semites used this fact as a means of propaganda. In the trial that followed the murder, Mortiz Scharf, the I 3 year old son of the Synagogue porter, testified that he had peeked through the keyhole of the Synagogue door and had seen the Jews kill a Christian girl. It was soon demonstrated that the part of the Synagogue in which the crime was supposed to have been committed could not be seen through a keyhole. After the accused were freed, it finally turned out that the real murderer was a Christian nobleman who had impregnated the girl.

The public, however, was goaded into believing the ritual murder accusation. Geza Von Onody, a deputy in the Hungarian Diet, organised anti-Semitic opinion on a vast scale. Large mass meetings were held all over Hungary, followed by pillage and pogroms.

Nevertheless in this case the whole truth became known. Merits Scharf was exposed as a liar, and the coroner's report indicated that not the slightest trace of blood had been withdrawn from the body. At the close of the trial the States Attorney made the following statement:

"From the President's remarks I feel justified in concluding that the Supreme Court has always preferred to dispense with ritual murder accusations. I shall do the same and I am happy to do it. Even though the Rohlings will continue to brood over misquotations from the Talmud and have nightmares of bloody sacrifices, this expose of ritual murder, this absurd offspring of medieval superstition, this stupid subject of nursery tales and gossip of old village wives, puts an end to such nonsense forever in Hungary. . . I am completely convinced that all the defendants present are not guilty of the crime of which they have been accused ... I declare them innocent and ask the court to set them free immediately."

Judgment was passed on August 3, 1883. All were set free. The verdict of "not guilty" was confirmed by higher authorities.

One of the most spectacular cases of the last century took place in Kiev. In March, 1911 a 12-year old boy by the name of Jusczynski was murdered. Innumerable knife wounds were found on the corpse. The child had been playing at the home of a school chum whose mother was the leader of a gang of thieves. Suspicion fell on this woman. In the course of the trial an anti-Semitic student, Golubew, informed the Judge that this boy had been playing with the murdered child in a brick yard and that they were chased away by a man "with a black beard." On the basis of this testimony Mendel Beilis, an employee of the brick yard was arrested. He was kept in official custody for two years. The court took an inimical position and the ministers of justice tried to convert the hazy evidence into a ritual murder process. The criminal lawyers who had protested Beilis' innocence were dismissed and called to account. One of his defenders was censured by the court, and legal proceedings were instituted against another attorney for alleged perjury. The trial was delayed at the order of higher-ups because the composition of the jury was not satisfactory to the State. The trial finally began on October 8, 191 3 and lasted until November 10 of the same year. The accusation was supported by two testimonies, one from Reverend Prinartus, a Catholic curate from Turkistan, who had written "The Christian in the Talmud", a work based on the material of Rohling and Justus, the other from Professor Sikorski of Kiev. Even before the trial took place well known scholars from other countries denounced these testimonies. Among the authorities who testified during the trial were Professor Kokovziev and the Muscovite, Rabbi Mase, who denied the accusation. It soon became apparent that all the accusing witnesses had to offer was assumptions. No evidence could be established. Despite the prevalent anti-Semitic propaganda and its influence on public opinion, the court, consisting of eleven peasants, was not convinced of Beilis' guilt, and he was set free. This case aroused the entire European world. Outstanding public figures vehemently condemned the ritual murder legend. On March 12, 191 3, a protest was made in Berlin by 215 famous Germans, among them brilliant scholars, deputies, clerics, authors and artists. They stated that there had never been the slightest proof to justify this insane indictment of Jewry. They declared, furthermore, that highly respected Christian scholars of the Jewish Scriptures have testified that the Jewish religion has never instructed its communicants to murder their fellow men.

On May 7, 1912 an English protest against ritual murder accusations was signed by the Archbishop of Canterbury, several bishops of the Church of England, the Dukes of Norfolk and Northumberland, Lord Arthur James Balfour and Sir Austen Chamberlain.

CHAPTER 8

Jewish Idealism and self-Sacrifice

Hitler maintains that the Jews never possessed a culture of their own, but always borrowed their intellectual substance from other peoples. He contends that "even if the Jews' drive for self-preservation is greater than that of other peoples and even if their mental abilities would give the impression that they are the intellectual equals of other races, they completely lack the most essential prerequisite of a civilised people, that is, an idealistic state of mind ... The will to self-sacrifice in the Jewish people does not transcend a sheer drive for self-preservation ... If the Jews were alone in this world, they would live in filth and would exploit and annihilate one another in a battle of hate, unless their inevitable lack of self-sacrifice, as expressed by their proverbial cowardice, would transplant the battle to the theatre."

These Hitlerian comments on cowardice, lack of idealism and of self-sacrifice in the Jews are totally devoid of any truth.

Count Heinrich von Coudenhove-Kalergi devoted more than seventy pages of his "Essence of Anti-Semitism" to the persecution of the Jews. On page 168 of this book, he tells us that: "Those Jews who steadfastly bore all these miseries were not very wise. Like so many of their co-religionists they apparently could have gone over to Christianity and secretly observed the Mosaic faith; but they did not do that and consequently suffered. In this respect they did not act very shrewdly, and I sincerely regret their attitude. Their perseverance, however, required such colossal heroic courage, such superhuman greatness and such majesty of character that I must bow to these sufferers in deep respect and in boundless admiration, crying instead of 'Jude, Jude, Hep, Hep, Hep' (German rabble cry against the Jew), 'Judea, Judea, Hip Hip, Hooray!' "

On page 278 of his book Coudenhove-Kalergi writes:

"I must confess that of my Christian friends and acquaintances, I know of only three who were Semi-tophiles. Furthermore, I must say that I myself was once a theoretical anti-Semite. In my younger years I was even a practical anti-Semite, owing to my unpleasant experiences with Jewish usurers. Several years ago when I decided to make a study of the Jewish question, if someone would have asked me whether my report would be anti-Semitic, I probably would have answered in the affirmative. A serious and thorough study of the matter has taught me otherwise. I feel that I have rendered a service to the Jews as well as to the anti-Semites in presenting both with the evidence that anti-Semitism is based on religious fanaticism. Yes, it is just those anti-Semites who ought to be convinced that they are guilty of an egregious error in making the Jews responsible for a whole series of political and social misdemeanors of which they are entirely innocent. If the anti-Semites about-face and seek the real causes, they will probably find them ... I would be very grateful to my opponents if they point out any errors I might have made. If they can correct my mistakes, I am open to conviction. But I must demand only scientific information from my critics, because I cannot consider assumptions or aspersions as counter-evidence.

"Let us all cooperate in putting an end to anti-Semitism, this monstrous relic of medievalism, which deserves to die. We are faced with many problems in these days of progress the most important of which is the outlawing of war by means of an international arbitrary court. Others are to improve working conditions, to aid the poor and to alleviate their miseries."

Shortly before his death Coudenhove-Kalergi wrote:

"... Dependent upon no one and blessed not too well with earthly goods, I asked only for the privilege of writing in order to serve the interests of truth. I regarded myself as a servant to everyone who sought the truth, free from prejudice and assumptions."

The testimony of Count Coudenhove-Kalergi is not my only means of refuting Hitler's accusations. I have at my disposal important events in the past and present history of the Jews, a survey of which suffices to prove the fortitude and heroism of this people.

It is most deplorable that those peoples with anti-Semitic

prejudices, particularly the Germans, who are concerned about the cultural significance of most things, are completely ignorant of the history of one of the oldest and most civilised peoples in the world. With the exception of a few sincere Christian scholars, it is usually the anti-Semites who browse around for material on the Jews. They can always profit by the omnipresent ignorance of Jewish history.

I cannot depict the entire history of Israel within these few pages. I can only select several episodes from Graetz;, "History of the Jews," (1923) to support my avowal that the Israelites have always been a brave people.

At the time of the war between the Hebrews and the Philistines, King Saul and his army were encamped scarcely an hour's distance from the enemy. Between both camps interposed a narrow gorge, surrounded by steep perpendicular cliffs and slopes which narrowed down to a chasm scarcely ten feet wide. The Philistines and the Israelites could approach one another only in a roundabout way. Jonathan, one of Saul's army commanders, and his warriors set out to climb the steep wall of the cliff at the narrowest spot in the pass. A mis-step would have meant a sudden drop to the ground and death. Fortunately they all succeeded in reaching the top. When the Philistines saw these courageous men, they derided them. The Hebrews drew closer and pelted the Philistines with rocks. The latter retreated in confusion, and their ranks broke up into wild flight.

The single combat of young David with the giant Goliath is a great historical event. Yet David was not a warrior but a shepherd, who had been entrusted by his father with a message to his brothers serving in the Israelite army.

When Saul was besieged by the heavy cavalry and war chariots of the Philistines, he did not care to flee or be taken prisoner by the Philistines. He fell upon his own sword and died in the manner worthy of a king.

During a lull in the battle, King David expressed a desire to drink water from a cistern in Bethlehem which was then in the possession of the Philistines. Three of his men immediately set out for Bethlehem. Arriving there, they frightened away the Philistines by their dauntless valor, fetched the water from the cistern and brought it to the King. David venerated the water, because these heroes had brought it to him at the risk of their lives.

Sometime after the Greek conquest of Judea, Antiochus Epiphanes tried to force the Judaeans to relinquish their own faith and accept idol-worship. The Judaeans offered resistance and were severely persecuted.

"When the bloody persecution of the Judaean people had reached such a height that either the destruction of the whole nation, or their submission from exhaustion and despair seemed imminent, an open rebellion took the place of passive resistance.

"It was brought about by a family whose members combined the purest piety with courage, wisdom and prudence; this was the family of the Hasmonaeans or Maccabees. An aged father and five heroic sons brought about a revolution, and kindled a spirit of enthusiasm which secured the existence of Judaism for all time. The aged father, Mattathias, had left Jerusalem in consequence of the desecration of the Temple, and had established himself in the small town of Modin, three miles north of Jerusalem. His five sons, who all helped to raise the people from its deep degradation, and found their death in defending their country, bore Aramaic names: Johanan Gadi, Simon Tharsi, Judas Maccabi, Eleazar Hawran, and Jonathan Haphus. This family of Hasmonaeans, who had many followers, on account of the consideration in which they were held, felt the miserable condition of their country with poignant sorrow. 'What is life to us, now that the Sanctuary is desecrated and Judea has become a slave?' Thus spoke Mattathias to his sons, and he determined not to remain quiet and sorrowing in his hiding-place, but either to help the good cause or to die courageously for it.

"When Apelles, one of the Syrian overseers, reached Modin, to summon the inhabitants to abandon the Law and to become idolaters, Mattathias and his sons intentionally appeared, and when commanded to set an example of submission, the former answered: 'If all the people in the kingdom obey the order of the monarch, to depart from the faith of their fathers, I and my sons will abide by the Covenant of our forefathers.' When one of the Judaeans approached the altar to sacrifice to Jupiter, Mattathias could no longer restrain his wrath, but rushed upon the apostate, killing him at the altar. His sons, armed with long knives, fell upon Apelles and his troops, killed them and destroyed the altar. This act proved the turning-point; it set an example of courageous resistance as against inactive despair. Immediately after this attack upon the officers of Antiochus, Mattathias cried out: 'Whosoever is zealous for the Law, and whosoever wishes to support the Covenant, follow me.' Thereupon the inhabitants of Modin and the vicinity followed him to a secure hiding-place which he selected for them in the mountains of Ephraim; and there the remainder of the Chasidim, who had escaped death in the caves, and all those who had fled from oppression joined him.

"The number of resolute defenders of their country daily increased ... Mattathias waged a kind of petty warfare against the enemy, such as can be carried on only in mountainous districts, but may wear out the most powerful enemy. When the death of the aged Mattathias drew nigh, he designated Judas as the commander of the army . . . Judas Maccabeus was a warrior such as the House of Israel had not known since the time of David and Joab, than whom he was nobler and purer . . . Invisible strength seemed to emanate from his hero-soul, which imbued all who surrounded him with the same dauntless courage. He was endowed with the instincts of a general, and this enabled him to fight at the right moment, to take advantage of his enemy's weakness, and to deceive him by means of feigned attacks. In the hour of battle, 'he was like a lion in his rage,' and when at rest, like a dove in gentleness and simplicity ..."

"Antiochus commissioned Lysias to march against Judea with the troops left in his charge, and, after conquering the Judaeans, to destroy and uproot every remnant of Israel and every trace of Jerusalem; and the land was to be colonised by foreign tribes, and divided among them ... In every town, and in every country, where the king's commands became known, great terror filled the hearts of the Judaeans, and they fasted and wept. The Elders dressed themselves in their penitential garb, and lay in ashes. But this unprecedentedly cruel plan of destroying a whole people, men, women and children, roused new champions for the defense of their country . . .

"Antiochus sent his general, Georgias, with 40,000 men to Judea. Georgias was so certain ofvictory that he invited slave-traders to come into his camp, and to bring with them money and chains. The Syrian commander thought that it would be more prudent to sell the captives as slaves than to kill them; but whilst he was thus prematurely disposing of them, the Judaean warriors, numbering 6,000, assembled round Judas Maccabeus. Before leading them into action, the commander, in order to animate them with the spirit of heoric self-sacrifice, organized a solemn assembly in the mountain city ofMizpah ... The assembly was deeply moved; all its members observed a strict fast during the day, wore mourning garments, and prayed with all the fervour of their sorrowing hearts for help and compassion . . . Judas issued a proclamation to the effect that all those who were newly married, who had built a house or planted a new vineyard, or who lacked sufficient courage, were permitted to withdraw from the ranks . . . The Syrian leader wished to surprise the Judaeans in the night, but was outwitted by Maccabeus. As soon as night set in, Judas left the camp with his followers, marched by well-known roads to the west, and came upon the enemy's rear. When Georgias found the camp of the Judaeans deserted, he imagined that fear had driven them into the mountains, and he pursued them thither. This was the object of Judas- stratagem. He followed the Syrians, reached their camp, set it on fire, and pursued the troops . . . The Judaean army was greater in number than the single division of Syrian troops, and fought with great enthusiasm. Thus the enemy was beaten, and put to flight . . . The victory crippled the enemy, and inspired the Judaeans with confidence in their own power. Neither the cavalry nor the foot-soldiers, with their helmets and shields, alarmed them any longer. The victors returned to their meeting-place at Modin with songs of rejoicing. ... In the following year (.16 5), when Lysias attacked Judea with a powerful, picked army of cavalry and foot-soldiers, he found the Judaeans more courageous and determined than ever . . . Maccabeus marched with his 10,000 men to meet him; a regular battle ensued, in which the impetuous attacks of the Judaeans again secured a victory over the strategy of the Syrian hirelings. Lysias departed, furious at his defeat." (Graetz;, Vol. I, pages 458-470).

A war began again in 162 B. C. It was an unfavorable time for the Judaeans because it was the Sabbatical year which was strictly observed by those who were ready to forfeit their lives for the law. There was neither sowing nor reaping and the people had to maintain themselves with the foods of the trees. The garrisons of the fortresses could not be supplied with sufficient food.

Lysias at the head of a large army with elephants marched toward the south side of Judea. Judas Maccabeus could send only a small army into the field. Lysias moved on to Jerusalem, and Maccabeus met him on the field. The Jews again performed prodigies of valor. Eliezer, one of the Hasmonean brothers, crawled under an elephant, believing that the magnificently attired rider was the King himself, stabbed the animal to death and fell crushed by its enormous weight. But, in spite of the courage and daring of the Judaeans, they were obliged to retreat before the superior numbers of the Syrians. Judas Maccabeus returned to Jerusalem and there entrenched himself and his army in the Temple fortress. Lysias soon followed and besieged the sanctuary. The siege continued for a long time and as supplies were not plentiful, they were soon consumed by the garrison. Tortured by hunger, the troops began to desert the fortress through subterranean passages. Only Judas Maccabeus, his three brothers and a small band of devoted followers remained steadfastly at their post of danger defying their pangs of hunger.

Help came unexpectedly when Lysias was threatened by a new opponent. He was forced to make peace with the Judaeans, granting them complete religious freedom and the inviolation of the fortress of the Temple. Because of his heroic deeds Judas Maccabeus was raised to the high priesthood.

Several years later the Syrian King Demetrius sent the leader of his elephant troop, Nicanor, to proceed against the insurgents with the utmost harshness. Having heard of the valor and heroism of Judas Maccabeus, Nicanor desired to effect a reconciliation between Judas Maccabeus and the King. Nicanor was so enchanted with the Judaean hero that he advised him, after the conclusion of peace negotiations, to take a wife and bring an heroic race into the world. But the King sent strict orders to Nicanor to cease all negotiations and to send Judas in chains to Antiochus. Judas retreated to the mountains where he was followed by Nicanor and his army. He renewed hostilities with untiring energy, his chief object being to take Judas prisoner. In order to induce the Judaeans to surrender, Nicanor ordered that, the most respected man in Jerusalem, the Ragesh or Razis, be seized and kept as a hostage, but the latter committed suicide.

Meanwhile, Judas had collected together 3,000 of his previous followers. Judaean valor was again triumphant over the superior numbers of the Syrians. Nicanor fell on the battlefield and his army fled in utter confusion. This battle was so decisive that its anniversary was afterwards celebrated. At this juncture Judas, foreseeing that Demetrius would avenge the destruction of his army, made overtures to the all-powerful State of Rome, a doubtful strategy. Demetrius, upon hearing of Nicanor's defeat, sent an immense army headed by the merciless Bacchides, to Judea. Judas issued a proclamation to the men and youths of Judea to come forth and fight for their fatherland, their law and their freedom. 3,000 responded to the call. Bacchides followed the Jewish army with 20,000 foot and 2,000 mounted soldiers.

Selecting the most valiant of his small number Judas successfully attacked the right wing of Bacchides and drove the enemy far back. But the miniature troop of Judaean soldiers left behind unable to withstand the desperate onslaught of the left wing of the Syrian army was routed. When Judas returned from the pursuit, he was obliged to resume battle with the Syrians. He and his band of picked men performed wonders of bravery. On both sides fell the dead and the wounded, and the battle lasted from morning to evening. The Judaean army became smaller and smaller and its survivors were entirely surrounded by the enemy. At last even Judas Maccabeus fell, sword in hand. The few remaining soldiers fled from the battlefield, the Maccabean brothers being fortunate enough to save the body of their heroic commander from disgrace.

At the fall of Jerusalem under the Roman Emperor Titus the world again witnessed the heroic courage of the Jews. Before Titus besieged Jerusalem, he asked the inhabitants to peacefully open the gates of the city, but the valiant warriors refused to submit to his command. They had sworn to protect the city with their lives and would not surrender. Whereupon Titus laid waste all the vegetation about the north and the west of Jerusalem. When he reached the northern wall, the Judaeans suddenly emerged from a gateway and separated him from his retinue. They almost took him prisoner, but he was covered by some of his soldiers. Some time later when the tenth legion was installed at the Mount of Olives, they were suddenly fallen upon by the Judaeans and were so frightened that they dropped everything and fled. But these skirmishes were unsuccessful. The Judaeans were constantly obliged to retreat into the fortress; yet these brave expeditions convinced the Romans that they would have a serious battle in store for them. Battering rams were erected at three points along the walls to demolish them. As soon as the Romans had set up their machines, the Judaeans pushed forth like demons and destroyed them, dispersed the enemy in fear and confusion and again retreated behind the walls. All those who could bear weapons participated in the battles; even women showed an exemplary contempt for death. The besieged threw boulders or poured seething oil on the heads of their enemies. Gradually they learned how to use heavy artillery against the Romans. But oppressed by a stronger force, the Jews had to leave the outer walls. There began a heated battle over the second walls which the defenders had erected behind the first. The Romans attempted to destroy these walls, but the Judaeans, commanded by Jochanan, gained access to the war machines by means of a subterranean passage and destroyed them. With danger close by, the courage of the besieged increased. They knew what to expect from the Romans. Titus had 500 prisoners crucified in one day. Others he sent back with hands chopped off. Titus wanted to give up the siege when he was joined by a powerful ally — famine. After a prolonged period, the Romans succeeded in capturing the second wall but were shocked to find still another wall. They attempted to take the wall by storm but the attack was warded off by the Judaeans. In vain did Titus demand that the city surrender. He even promised to spare the Temple. Meanwhile the angel of destruction spread famine throughout the population of Jerusalem and sapped the very energy of the people, lifting the barriers between rich and poor. The warriors bore this hardship with undaunted courage. They advanced to the attack as starving men, surrounded by the dismal picture of death. Yet they went with the same enthusiasm as on the first day of the siege. The Romans stood in admiration before the death-defying and unflinching courage of these heroes. They considered them invincible. Several Romans left their banners and their belief and went over to the Judaeans. The inhabitants of Jerusalem were so proud of this conversion at the hour of greatest danger that they saw to it that the converts did not starve. The enemy attacked the outer walls of the Temple and for six days fought incessantly without being able to destroy them. Finally a Roman soldier seized a burnt torch, was boosted up by a companion and threw it through the golden window of the Temple. The flames rose high. At this sight the most courageous were taken aback. The maddened soldiers forced their way into the Temple. Titus wanted to see the Holy of Holies but the choking smoke drove him out. Again the Jewish warriors pushed forward. A new battle took place at the scene of conflagration. But the sea of fire was an omen to the inhabitants that all hope was lost. Many Judaeans in sheer desperation jumped into the flames. They did not want to live beyond the Temple. Thousands of others, men, women and children, remained within the walls of the Temple despite the hovering enemy and the searing fire. The Romans advanced and felled them. Several priests caught on the walls were executed by Titus. The battle still waged. The Judaeans retreated into the upper city. There they had a conference with Titus. Since they had sworn to die rather than to surrender, they demanded that they be allowed to retire with their weapons. Titus demanded that they surrender unconditionally. And so the battle started anew. The Romans began to attack the upper city. They rose above the walls and forced their murderous way into the city which they burned for days. With the exception of three towers left untouched, the city was levelled to the ground and its brave population annihilated.

How do the Nazis reconcile these heroic deeds of the Jews with accusations of cowardice and lack of self-sacrifice?

"From the very beginning," writes Hitler, "The Jew could not possess a religious attitude because he was utterly without idealism."

The Nazis tell us that the Jews seek only pleasure. Hitler himself claims that "the Talmud is not for the other world but only for a practical and endurable life in this world."

It is true that Judaism as a religion does not despise the acquisition and enjoyment of earthly goods. It wants man to enjoy life. Therefore monasticism could never originate on Jewish soil. Yet concessions made to the flesh were regulated by a strict code of laws, the purpose of which is climaxed in the following sentence from Leviticus 19: "Ye shall be holy: for I the Lord your God am holy". Actually we find in the Jewish tenets of faith a temperance and a moral purity. The Tenth Commandment reads: "Thou shalt not covet thy neighbor's wife, neither shalt thou covet thy neighbor's house, his field, or his man-servant, or his maidservant, his ox or his ass, or anything that is thy neighbor's."

According to Leviticus 23, 24, and 25, the Jewish religion forbids the sale of ground for eternal possession and ordains that every five years a new division of the acres based on the increase in population should take place, making it impossible for one family to inherit fortune and power. When we compare this agrarian legal code with the Germanic feudal system, whose last remnants are still incorporated in the feoffment trust, we wonder whether the Jews deserve to be reproached for materialism. Deuteronomy 17: 16 and 17, forbids the king to procure many horses and accumulate gold and silver.

In I Kings 3:9,11, Solomon asks not for wealth but for wisdom, and in Proverbs 30:8, he implores: "Give me neither poverty nor riches; feed me with food convenient for me."

"Labor not to be rich: cease from thine own wisdom." (Proverbs 23:4)

"A faithful man shall abound with blessings: but he that maketh haste to be rich shall not be innocent." (Proverbs 28:20)

"There is a grievous evil which I have seen under the sun, namely, riches, kept for the owners thereof to their hurt." (Ecclesiastes 5:13)

"As the partridge sitteth on eggs, and hatcheth them not; so he that getteth riches, and not by right, shall leave them in the midst of his days, and at his end shall be a fool." (Jeremiah 17:11)

Their history, let alone their religion, tells us that the Jews as a people never strived for wealth or power. Close as they were to the coast and to the Phoenicians, they made few attempts to go to sea. Israel modestly confined itself to the defense of its borders and its religion.

Isaiah II called the Babylonians "gold hoarders." Both this prophet (Chapter 23) and Ezekiel (Chapter 17) attacked Tyrus and Sidon for their wanton craving for gold and luxury. Since they did not attribute this craving to their own nation, we may assume that it did not exist there. For the prophets never hesitated to point out the failings of their own people. (Stern, Die Lehrsätze des neugermanischen Judenhasses 1879, page 12.— "The Principles of Modern German Anti-Semitism.")

Whoever seeks the epitome of idealism and self-sacrifice should follow the tragic history of the Jews during the Middle Ages. The following episodes from Graetz; are more than sufficient to disprove the anti-Semitic concoctions of the Nazis. Do we, who have broken every tenet of the Christian faith in our treatment of the Jews, have any right to criticize them? Christians have robbed, murdered and falsely testified against the Jews, not a thousand years ago, but less than two hundred years ago. The crimes of which the Nazis accuse the Jews, if true, would be negligible compared to the atrocities and brutalities they have committed upon the Jews. Judaism was founded on idealism and self-sacrifice.

The first Crusaders did not molest the Jews considerably. But the following throngs murdered and plundered them ruthlessly. Attempts were made to convert the Jews forcibly to Christianity. Up to this time massacres had been committed only in France. For the first time the persecutions on German soil assumed a particularly tragic character. When the Jewish community of Trier heard that the Crusaders were approaching, it was seized by such panic that parents killed their own children and themselves. Women and girls tied stones to their garments and threw themselves into the Mosel to avoid compulsory conversion and rape. The Crusaders moved on to Speier. Here they dragged ten Jews into the church and on pain of death tried to force them to conversion.

They steadfastly refused to be converted, and all were executed on May 3, 1096. The remaining Jews took refuge in the palace of Bishop Johanson and in the castle of the Emperor. The Bishop, who did not believe in such conversion, sent his guards to meet the maddened throng. In Worms Bishop Allebrandus hid many Jews in his palace. The others succumbed to the blows of the Crusaders. Many committed suicide. Women slew their own children. After seven days the mob went after those who had found protection in the episcopal palace. The leaders demanded that they renounce their belief. Allebrandus was powerless. The Jews asked for a brief respite to deliberate the matter. The Crusaders waited before the palace to lead the Jews either to the church or to death. When the pause was ended and the Bishop went to ask the Jews about their decision, he found all of them swimming in blood. They had killed one another.

In Mainz the Archbishop invited the Jews to take refuge in his palace until the storm was over. Thirteen hundred of them entrusted their wealth to him and lay with heavy hearts in fervent prayer. At the break of dawn the Crusaders appeared and with wild tumult demanded that the Jews be delivered to them. They easily broke down the doors of the palace and fell upon the Jews but found only corpses. The unfortunates had stabbed one another to death. I 300 corpses were removed from the palace. The Archbishop also had hidden sixty Jews in the cathedral, but they were seized and executed. Two men and two girls, Uria, Isaac and his two daughters, who out of weakness or confusion renounced their religion, were driven to a horrible deed by remorse. Isaac slew his daughters and set fire to his home. Thereafter he and his companion set fire to the Synagogue, and both died within the flames. In Cologne the Jews implored the burghers and the Bishop to protect them. Many humane burghers opened their homes to them. Bishop Herman III allowed the Jews to leave Cologne secretly and seek protection in towns and villages under his rule. But the Crusaders sought them out and slaughtered them. Many committed suicide in lakes and swamps. A learned old man, Samuel Ben Uchiel, set an example to the others. He killed his handsome young son and himself on a river bank and both fell into the water with an "Amen." Those standing about joined in the prayer and then threw themselves into the water. All in all, more than 12,000 Jews were killed within the space of two months in the Rhineland. When the Crusaders came to Bohemia, that country was engaged in war. Thus they had complete freedom to drag the Jews to conversion and to kill those who resisted. In vain did the Bishop preach against these outrages.

The Jews in Jerusalem were horribly persecuted. Alter the Crusaders had taken the Holy City by storm and bathed the Mohammedans in blood, they drove the Jews into the Synagogue, set fire to it and sent them all to a dreadful death (1099.) The Second Crusade brought even more tribulations to the Jews. Rudolph, an eloquent monk, inflamed the fanatical Germans against the Jews. He thought he was performing a pious deed by offering the unbelievers conversion or complete annihilation. In August, 1146, the first victims fell. One man, Simon the Pious, refused to be converted and was mutilated and murdered. A woman known as Mina of Speier, who had suffered indescribable torture at

the rack, still remained true to her faith. Cardinal Arnold promised protection to the Jews. He even took them into his home, but they were murdered before his eyes. An energetic protest made by the famous Abbot Bernard of Clairvaux was ineffectual. The Abbot stated therein that the "Jews are not to be disturbed or destroyed because they are living symbols of the Passion; for which they are to be punished mainly by dispersion, so that they shall be witnesses.
But they will ultimately be converted. How can this be if they are ground down?"

Bernard's attempts to control the mobs were all in vain. When the remains of a Christian were found in Würzberg, the Jews were accused of ritual murder (1147)- More than twenty Jews suffered a martyr's death, among them an outstanding Rabbi who was murdered while reading the Holy Scriptures. Sympathetic Christians took care of the wounded, namely, those who had been overlooked as dead.

The Jews had to wear a badge to differentiate them from Christians and thereby became the objects of scorn for the upper classes and targets of abuse for the lower classes. The following centuries brought the Jews more persecution and torture. They were burdened with the entire fury of medieval society and reduced to pitiable figures.

Degradation did not seem enough. The Jews were considered pariahs to be killed without the slightest qualms of conscience, like mad dogs. Every conceivable crime was ascribed to them and always found credence. They were accused so often of mutilating Christian children that even well-meaning people began to believe this mesh of lies.

It is impossible to depict all the shocking events that took place in the Middle Ages within the space of this book. Most of them arose from accusations of ritual murder, of desecration of the Host and of poisoning the wells. After confessions had been extracted from Jews at the rack, and they were subsequently executed, it soon became known that they were innocent and that these accusations were based upon lies and calumnies.

A Spaniard by the name of Juan Vero, who had words with a Jew, had the freshly buried corpse of a Christian exhumed, placed in the home of his Jewish enemy and the grave filled with stones. When rumor was spread that the body of a Christian was found in a Jewish home, scores of Jews were robbed and murdered in the cities of Ecia and Palma. Upon hearing of this, the King offered a prize of 500 gold pieces to anyone who immediately could present him with the facts of the situation. A servant of Juan Vero reported the deed of his master and when the grave was examined, only stones were found. Juan and his accomplice were executed.

A Jew was once accused of having murdered a Christian by the name of Guzman for blood ritual purposes. He confessed the deed on the rack and was condemned to death. Just as judgment was to be carried out, the bishop of that locality asked why the Jew was to be executed. On hearing the charge, he stated that he knew Guzman personally and had seen him several days ago in a village close by. Guzman was sent for and appeared in person before the king. The king thereafter decreed that the rack was never to be used again.

In Holy Week of 1475 a three-year old child, named Simon was drowned in the Adige, and the corpse was caught in a grating close to the house of a Jew. Anticipating misrepresentation of the event, he hurried to Bishop Hinderback to give him notice of the occurrence. The bishop took two men of high position with him, went to the place and had the body carried into the Church. As soon as the news spread, hostile priests raised a fierce outcry against the Jews, saying that they had tortured and slain the child and then flung it into the water. The body of the child was exhibited, in order to inflame the fury of the populace against them. The bishop had all the Jews of Trent, high and low, cast into prison, commenced proceedings against them and called a physician to testify to the violent death of the child. The imprisoned Jews confessed under torture that they had slain Simon and drunk his blood on the night of the Passover. Only one of the tortured victims, a man named Moses, endured every torment without confirming the lying accusations of his enemies. The result was that all the Jews of Trent were burnt, and it was resolved that no Jew should thenceforth settle in the city.

The corpse of the child was embalmed and commended to the populace as a holy relic. It was imperative that the marvel be believed in, and so the Jews of all Christian countries were jeopardized anew. Even in Italy they dared not go outside the towns lest they be slain as child-murderers.

The doge, Pietro Mocenigo, and the Venetian senate, on the complaint of the jews about the insecurity of their lives and property, issued orders to the podesta of Padua to defend them against fanatical outbreaks, and to forbid the preaching friars to inflame the mob against them. The doge accompanied the orders with the remark that the rumor that Jews had slain a Christian child in Trent was a fabrication, a device invented by their enemies to serve some purpose. When Pope Sixtus IV was urged to canonize little Simon he steadfastly refused, and sent a letter to all the towns of Italy, on October 10th, 1475, forbidding Simon of Trent to be honored as a saint until he could investigate the matter, and thus he allayed the popular excitement against the Jews.

All this the Jews suffered because of their belief. It is a fact that during the Middle Ages every Jew had the choice of renouncing his belief, therewith humiliation and torture, and becoming an equal member of society. For remaining true to their faith despite horrible persecution, the Jews deserve the greatest admiration. During this trying period they thought little of wealth, power or the exertion of political influence. In their prayers, those laments that would soften hearts of stone, they ask only for a place to lay their weary heads, for God to save their lives and allow them to observe their religion in peace. In "Oh Weep For Those" from his "Hebrew Melodies" Lord Byron expressed his deep sympathy for the Jews in euphonius poetic form:

"Tribes of the wandering foot and weary breast,
How shall ye flee away and be at rest?
The wild dove hath her nest, the fox his cave,
Mankind their country—Israel, the grave."

That idealism was always predominant in the Jewish character and that the Jews always appreciated human values, truth and social justice are illustrated in the following passages from Graetz.

When King Saul conquered the Amalekites and took King Agag prisoner, the Israelite warriors found rich booty. According to the decree of the Prophet Samuel, this wealth was not to be used but to be destroyed. Because the warriors would not give up the booty and because Saul, ordinarily so rigid in his discipline, permitted the preservation of the booty and thus transgressed the Prophet's directions, the latter said to him: "Because thou hast rejected the Word of the Lord, He hath also rejected thee from being King." He added the following in winged words: "God hath as much delight in obedience as in sacrifice and burnt offerings. Behold, to obey is better than sacrifice and to harken better than the fat of rams." Saul's disobedience brought him great sorrow and led to the loss of his throne.

The deeds of the Prophet Elijah, at the end of the **10th** Century B. C. are known everywhere. Elijah would have given up his life for his convictions without the slightest hesitation. He was the embodiment of religious and moral zeal. Like a storm he roared at King Ahab, thundered violent words at him and like a storm subsided.

Unlike the luxuriously garbed idol-worshipping prophets, he wore a simple black hair-cloth garment with a leather belt. He abstained from wine, was opposed to voluptuousness and love of pleasure, and stood for simplicity and temperance. He and his disciples waged mighty wars against the priests of Baal. Queen Isabel had many of these disciples executed without clemency. When King Ahab ordered a neighbor killed in order to confiscate his property, Elijah suddenly appeared before him and cried out: "Hast thou murdered and now seizeth possession? God saw the innocently spilled blood yesterday. Thou shalt suffer punishment for this on this very field"—and Ahab suffered a horrible death. The members of Elijah's school of prophets kept their hands free of alms and lived simply and abstemiously by their own work. They were brave and despised death. Their task was to prevent the Israelites from reverting to idol-worship. One hundred years after the ministry of the Prophet Elijah his prophetic disciples carried on with his zeal and with his spirit. The Jewish youth, quite receptive to ideals, reviled the manner of living of the rich, who opposed the poor. It came to the point where children arose against their parents. Significant is the curse of the Prophet Amos who, as a simple shepherd, attacked the perversity of the times. "Forasmuch therefore as your treading is upon the poor, and ye take from him burdens of wheat: ye have built houses of hewn stone, but ye shall not dwell in them; ye have planted pleasant vineyards, but ye shall not drink wine of them."

The Prophet Isaiah possessed the courage which calls vice and crime by their right names, and which mercilessly brands the guilty. He surpassed all his predecessors in depth of thought, beauty of rhythm, exaltation of poetical expression, in the accuracy of his similes and in the clearness of his prophetic vision. Isaiah s eloquence combined simplicity with beauty of speech, conciseness with intelligibility and biting irony with an inspiring flow of language. His energies were entirely directed to exposing wickedness, to warning and exhorting the nation and to holding before it the ideal of a future, to attain which it must strive with heart and soul. For more than forty years he pursued his prophetic ministration with untiring zeal and unshaken courage.

Isaiah did not content himself with inveighing against sin; he depicted a moral ideal, through the realisation of which men would find happiness and contentment. "The king shall not judge after the sight of his eyes, and shall not decide after the hearing of his ears." Isaiah treated with great contempt the hypocrisy which praises God with the lips whilst the heart is far from Him. He scorned still more the offering of sacrifices combined with baseness of thought and wickedness to deed. —(Isaiah 1:11, 13; 29: 13.)

Isaiah drew into his circle the thoughtful and susceptible, who became at once his disciples and his children. He instilled into them the virtues of gentleness, patience, and entire resignation to God. The members of the circle were called the "gentle ones." From Isaiah they learnt not to complain of poverty and spoliation but to bear suffering and wrong with faith in God and His dispensations. These "gentle ones" formed a special community, to which they devoted all their heart and mind and to which Isaiah and his successors looked forward as the national core and substance.

A people from whom sprang such prophets, such ethics, a people that has sacrificed itself for its faith, most assuredly cannot be designated as cowardly or devoid of idealism.

Today a new generation of Jews bears witness to the mendacity of Nazi indictments. The courageous behavior of the Jews during the World War serves as further testimony of their merit.

According to Dr. J. Kreppel in his "Juden und Judentum von Heute"—(Jews and Judaism of Today), the English Jews evinced the greatest patriotism during the World War as soldiers at the front and as citizens under war administration. At the outbreak of the war the number of English Jews in active service was relatively small (50 in the marines, 400 officers and soldiers in the army and 600 men in the reserve corp). Before general conscription was instituted in England, already 10,000 Jews were in service. The greatest number of these were volunteers. Of Australia's total population of 19,000 Jews, 1800 volunteered for service; of these 250 were killed in action. A striking example of Jewish enthusiasm was a brigade composed exclusively of young men of the Mosaic faith. This brigade presented the army with 80 officers for field service. There were also many Jewish physicians and nurses who took care of the wounded and sick. The personnel of one hospital was made up entirely of Jewish people. Lady Samuel, wife of the English Minister of the Interior, offered her country estate as a hospital and convalescent home. A Jewish sailor, William Stern, was drowned on one of the first vessels sunk during the war. Lt. Henry Quez, whose name stood at the top of a long casualty list, was the first Jewish officer killed in the Battle of the Aisne, September 1914- There was scarcely a regiment without Jews.

About 8,700 British Jews were killed in action.

Of these 316 were commissioned and 2,000 non-commissioned officers.

The Jews were frequently distinguished for bravery. An example ofJewish heroism was Captain Robert Gu, who won the treasured Victoria Cross. He received this distinction for outstanding bravery, initiative and decisiveness.

Sir John Monasch commanded the Australian troops at the western front and led them to victory after victory. A second Jewish officer who attained the position of general was H. J. Seligmann who saw the war through from beginning to end. All three sons of Leopold Rothschild were in active service. Major Evelin Rothschild fell in Palestine, and Captain Anthony Rothschild was wounded at Galipoli. The air force contained many outstanding and brave Jewish pilots.

The patriotism of the French Jews was exemplary. It is difficult to ascertain the exact number that participated in the war. It is known that Jews from every stratum of society fought for France. Scholars left their academic work and turned their knowledge to good account at the front. Charles Nordmann, an astronomer, when a recruit in the army, discovered a more exact method of aiming and by mathematical analysis determined the distance of the enemy's guns according to their sound. General Nivel greatly appreciated the ability of these scholars. Second Lieutenant Henry Abram, Professor at the Sorbonne, was made an officer of the Legion of Honor for his improvement of the wireless telegraph and his submarine war service record. Of 450 pupils graduated from the Poly technique in 1914, sixteen were Jews; of these four were killed in action and three wounded. Among the wounded was the son of the Chief Rabbi of Paris, Dr. Levy, who suffered severe lacerations. A twenty year old lieutenant, Pierre Hadamart, son of a famous mathematician, met an heroic death at Verdun.

Jewish barristers, physicians, scientists, artists and writers all hastened to the battlefield. Captain Halphen, a composer and lecturer, died of a disease contracted at the front. The dramatist, Henry Bernstein, won honors as a pilot. Pierre Mortie, editor of "GilBlas", was highly praised for his war record at the front and in the air corps in the Orient. The Grumbach family of Belfort had seven sons, two step-sons and two grandsons under the colors. In Paris the Dreyfuss family had eight sons, and Aaron Weil nine sons fighting for France. The loss of many children was a frequent occurrence. Major Mayer lost three sons; Madame Picard, a widow, also lost three sons. In the casualty list of French aces we find the name of James Henry Rothschild, Baron Günster, who fell at Yser. The French Jews seemed to excel in the air service, and many were engaged in tank warfare.

Of its total number of 65,000, the Jewish population of Algiers gave 10,000 men to the army. Ten per cent of these men were distinguished for bravery. The Algerian Jewish families were quite large. A certain Madame Lelouche had eight sons in active service. The Palikas family gave twenty-five of its members to the cause.

Of the French Jewish clergy, Rabbi Boris of Luneville fell at the beginning of the war, and Rabbi Wechsler, a well-known teacher of theology, died of a disease contracted in the trenches. Four rabbis who acted as chaplains at the front fell in the line of duty. Rabbi Abraham Bloch was killed by a hand grenade as he bent over a mortally wounded Christian, handing him a crucifix for which he had asked. The death of Rabbi Bloch has been depicted in a stirring manner by a Catholic priest, and its site has been marked by a monument erected to his memory. Two French rabbis received the Cross of the Legion of Honor, and nineteen were given honorable mention.

There were many courageous Jewish nurses in the French ranks. Mademoiselle Blanche Levy who won the Croix de Guerre for heroism, spent thirty-five months at the firing line and took care of the wounded during the heaviest bombardments. Mademoiselle Sophie Friedmann, head nurse of a hospital that was always a target for air raids, received the Medaille de France for outstanding bravery. One of the most inspiring instances of Jewish patriotism was that of old Monsieur Kahn of Luneville who ran toward the Germans on the battlefield with the French flag in his hand, crying "Vive La France!" as he fell riddled by bullets.

The Jews of Italy more than fulfilled their obligations to their country during the war. Despite their small number, they rallied patriotically to the cause. Several months after the outbreak of the war, a memorial service was held in the Trastevere Synagogue at Rome. Over the doors of the Synagogue stood in large letters "Honor And Glory To Those Who Sacrificed Their Lives For Their Fatherland." The interior was bedecked with black crepe, and the altar was draped with the Italian flag. Chief Rabbi Angelo Sacerdote called out the names of the heroes one by one, a stirring procedure. Outstanding were the names of Angelo Astrologe, Decio Pontecorvo, Gualtiero Vechio, Ippolito Segre, Georgio Levi and Alessandro di Veroli.

Of 68 million Germans, 12,500,000 participated in the war (18.38% of the total population). According to the last census taken in Germany before the War (1910), 555,000 out of 68 million Germans were listed as Jewish. This did not include foreign born Jews ineligible for war service. Of these 5 5 5,000 Jews, 96,000 or 17-3% saw active service. Thus every sixth German Jew was in the army. For every one hundred Jewish soldiers, 78 or nearly four-fifths of them were front-line fighters.

The Jewish population in Germany, thus, had proportionately fewer participants in the war than the non-Jewish population. Let us not forget that the age-structure of the Jews in Germany differed from that of the total population. Germans of retiring age were usually in ratio to Germans young enough for military service. They were drafted from the ages of eighteen to forty-five. Due to the constantly decreasing birth-rate among the German Jews, the young age classes eligible for service were smaller in number than the old age classes. Thus those at an age class no longer capable of bearing arms were relatively greater among the Jews than among the total population.

In estimating the percentage of Jews in the war, the proportion of the Jewish population in the cities and in the country must be considered. Three-fourths of the German Jews dwelt in cities, partiallarly in the large cities. The German town and country population, due to its greater number and physically more qualified men, gave more soldiers to the army than the urban population.

Of 96,000 Jewish soldiers, 10,000 or almost 11% volunteered for war service. The first Reichstag Deputy to be killed in the war was a Jew by the name of Frank. At least 12,000 German Jews were killed in action.

The anti-Semites pay little attention to statistics. Shortly after the war Dietrich Eckart, a publisher of an anti-Semitic Munich weekly, offered a prize of 1,000 Mark to anyone who could prove that one Jewish family had had three sons in the trenches for three weeks during the War. Rabbi Freund of Hanover thereupon presented Mr. Eckart with a list of twenty Jewish families of his congregation who fulfilled this requirement. When the donor of the prize refused to accept this proof, the Rabbi brought suit against him in Munich. In the course of the trial the plaintiff presented the court with a list of fifty Jewish families who had seven or eight sons in service, several of which had lost three sons. The defendant acknowledged these facts and reluctantly paid the prize of 1,000 Mark which the Rabbi gave to public charities.

The individual accomplishments of the German Jews in the War were no less than those of their Christian compatriots. 35,000 Jewish soldiers were decorated, 33,000 raised in rank and 2,000 became officers. This high number of officers is particularly noteworthy, because there were no Jewish officers in Germany before the War, and therefore they all rose by dint of merit from the fighting ranks.

In 1918 an anti-Semitic deputy in the Reichstag, with the complete approbation of his clique, made the following query: "Did you ever see a Jewish flier?" This question could have been answered by an accurate list of over 125 Jewish fliers who were later increased by forty. By this we mean fliers who engaged in warfare with the enemy. Thirty Jewish aces were killed, among them Wilhelm Frankl who won the Pour le merite and Iron Cross, and Lieutenant Weil who was frequently decorated.

Joseph Cypes, a goldsmith and teacher, recently died of complications arising from severe wounds acquired in the War. This Jew was the youngest German volunteer in the World War. In Constantinople, where he lived, he volunteered for war service at the age of thirteen. He was soon at the front where he suffered such injuries that both of his legs had to be amputated. He was greatly honored and decorated for extreme courage. After the war ended, he came to Germany an invalid. He became a teacher in the Breslau Technical School. In his leisure time Cypes occupied himself with the history of art, and was to be appointed director of an art museum. His students worshipped him, and in public life he enjoyed great respect. As to all German Jews, the Hitler revolution was a terrible blow to Joseph Cypes. The National Socialists tried to deprive this hero of his position but in vain, for even the Nazi students held their teacher in great esteem. The chairman of the Breslau City Council attempted to question the "authenticity " of Cypes-military record. He failed utterly. The Breslau Magistrate had to be satisfied with a reduction in the number of hours that Cypes taught. Several months later Cypes underwent a new operation, which the crude amputation of his legs necessitated, and died of a hemorrhage on the operating table.

"Der Schild," the official organ of the National Association of Jewish Front-Line Soldiers, published a special number on the 20th anniversary of the outbreak of the World War in which was stated "The youngest volunteer in the German army born in Germany, was a Jew from Koenigsberg by the name of Scheyer, who at the age of fourteen years and eleven months entered the army on August 26, 1914, and the oldest volunteer was our Jewish comrade, Lieutenant Adolf Stern, who at sixty-three years of age rallied to the flag. Also worthy of mention is Max Meltzer who at seventy years of age fought as a private together with his forty-four year old son Siegmund. Many Jewish families had from eight to ten sons in active service . . .

"Immediately after the outbreak of the War the Jews of Germany raised a fund and founded therewith a hospital at a cost of 130,000 Mark. By November 1, 1918 more than 6,000 Jews had volunteered for service. The first flag taken by the German army during the War was captured by a German-Jewish soldier named Fischel. 96,000 Jewish soldiers served in the German army; 12,000 were killed in action."

Yet, the Nazis call the Jews traitors, parasites, foreign bodies and enemies of Germany.

In Austria-Hungary the Jews not only saw active service but participated in welfare work and granted loans to the war administration. Emperor Franz; Joseph, and after him Emperor Karl, thanked the Jews on every possible occasion for their patriotism. The army leaders and commanders constantly expressed their appreciation of Jewish accomplishment on the field of honor.

Because of the collapse of the Dual Monarchy, it is impossible to estimate the number of Austrian and Hungarian Jews in the War. Nevertheless it is safe to say that they were present in proportion to their number among the total population. The fifty million subjects of the monarchy gave nine million soldiers (18%) to the army and navy. Since the Jews in Austria-Hungary amounted to 5% of the total population, their number in the war must have been over 400,000. No less than 474 Austrian-Jewish officers were killed in action. The accomplishments of Jewish soldiers were highly praised on different occasions. General von Dankl in a note to his Jewish men wrote: "You have all fought courageously in the Battle of Piotrokow on August 29th and have set a fine example to the troops. I hereby confer great praise upon you in the name of the Emperor."

Major Jambor, Royal Hungarian Local Militia, Regiment 14. sent the following note to the brother of Mr. Geza Kramer of Nytra: "Your brother, Lieutenant Geza Kramer, was killed in action at 8:00 PM., September 7th. His heroic death occurred in the zealous fulfillment of his duty as a campaign commander. His men bore his body into a barn near Godow. In retreating the company left the body behind. The enemy set fire to the barn. It may be a consolation to your honored family that the deceased conducted himself in every battle as a true hero with unflinching perseverance and with undaunted courage. He served every commander fully conscious of his duty, and set a worthy example to the others."

The National Association of Jewish Front-Line Fighters sent a request to the Generals of the old Austro-Hungarian army to comment on the attitude of Jewish soldiers and officers during the War. Such outstanding men as General-Majors Arz, Ernst Doming and G. von Järten, Generals Keppelmüller, von Sternschwerdt, Julius Kreischer, Karl Kikavszky and Julius Hoppe, Field Marshall Lieutenants R. von Gruber, E. von Krinnerstorff and Rudolph Pfeffer readily complied with this request. Said General Arz,: "I am happy to describe my experience with Jewish officers and soldiers at the front during the War. It gives me great satisfaction to state that they completely fulfilled their duties. Always ready, they fought with the greatest of devotion and bravery."

Said General Doming: "As a true Christian I have always had great sympathy for my Jewish compatriots and my many Jewish friends. In the World War I learned to know the Jews as diligent and good soldiers. In Troop 30 of the Hungarian Land Militia which I commanded I had many Jewish officers and soldiers under me, and again I must say that I have nothing but praise for them. They always rendered service equivalent to that of their fellow Christian officers and soldiers. In attacking Zugna Torta in the Southern Tyrol we had to take many prisoners in order to get information from them as to troop movements, plans of attack, etc. For this purpose I sent out patrols to capture Italian sentinels and small platoons. One of the outstanding members of these patrols was a Jewish buck-private named Goldstein. He was wounded several times and was decorated for exceptional bravery. But he was only one of numerous valiant Jewish fighters."

These answers all continue in the same vein of praise for Jewish courage and patriotism. Is it not strange, however, that those elements who stood furthest away from the firing line, are the ones who dare to call the Jews cowards and slackers?

The Jews of America were greatly devoted to their country during the War. It is quite difficult to estimate the exact percentage of American-Jewish War participants. New York State alone gave 50,000 Jewish soldiers. Reliable statisticians estimate that Jewish participation in the American World War forces was approximately double that which would have been justified by its proportions to the general American population. Twenty per cent of the Jews in the American army were volunteers, and sixty-seven per cent of the Jewish soldiers saw service at the firing line.

The American Jews received numerous citations for bravery. A Gentile captain, Henry Gen, said: "Approximately forty per cent of my division were Jews and how they fought! They made use of their astute mentality in battle. They looked for a hidden German battery so long and so hard until they found it." Major Whittley similarly remarked: "I have had an opportunity to become acquainted with many Jewish soldiers and to regard them with the greatest of admiration. Their heroic deeds are indelibly marked upon my memory." Many Jews won the highest honors that the United States bequeathed.

William Stableson was killed when he brought water to a thirsty buddy. Such instances were frequently reported by American officers. They contended that the great virtue of self-sacrifice was particularly manifest among the Jewish soldiers.

The total percentage of American Jews killed in action was approximately 3.500 or five per cent of the total loss of America. More than 2,000 Jews were wounded.

Joseph Trumpeldor was born 55 years ago in a Caucasian town. He died 15 years ago in the Palestinian colony of Tel Chai. His was indeed an heroic life. At the outbreak of the Russian-Japanese War, Trumpeldor entered the Czarist army as an ordinary private. He remained a private for a long time in spite of his heroic behavior. In the Czarist army a Jew could not become an officer very easily.

But Trumpeldor succeeded in breaking this anti-Semitic tradition. Once he seized the flag of his regiment from the hands of the Japanese; another time he saved the life of an Orthodox-Jewish Chaplain who lay wounded on the battle-field. During the siege of Port Arthur he was cited for bravery several times. One day a serious wound led to the amputation of his right arm. Trumpeldor's greatest problem then was that he could not carry a gun. As an invalid he was allowed to work in the étape behind the lines, but he wanted to remain at the front. He wanted to fight, even though Czarist Russia had not acted very kindly and Christian-like to his people. Trumpeldor knew only one thing. He was a soldier, and his country was at war. Therefore, he had to be among the first in the fighting Line, even though he had lost an arm.

The army commanders felt themselves obliged to raise him to the rank of officer. He was sent to the front again, this time as a lieutenant, and afterwards was taken prisoner by the Japanese. When the war was over, he returned to Russia where he received honor after honor. Even the anti-Semitism of the Czar was not so rabid as to undervalue the loyalty of a Trumpeldor. The "rejuvenators" of Germany ought to show that much sportsmanship.

After the War Trumpeldor went to Palestine as a pioneer, as one of the many thousands of young Jews who wanted to awaken their ancient, neglected barren homeland and to give it new life. The Chalutz; or the pioneer concept in the Jewish world of today owes its origin to Joseph Trumpeldor, for he created this pioneer movement in Russia. But, the hero of Port Arthur was not only an organizer; he was a man of action. So he became a Chalutz in the northern colony of Tel Chai. A second heroic period began in the life of Trumpeldor. It was heroism of a different sort, not on the battle-fields but in the tedium of civil life. It was the heroism of hard daily work on the earth of his forefathers for the generations to come. Trumpeldor was not destined to lead a peaceful life.

In January of 1920 the Arabian Druses led a revolt against French rule in Syria and in Lebanon. At that time the northernmost portion of Palestine — Galilee — was predominantly under French occupation. Thus the colony of Tel Chai, situated in this portion of the country, was involved in the turmoil. In their hatred of Europeans, the revolting Arabs made no distinction between the French soldiers and the peaceful Jewish workers. One day a troop of more than 3,000 Bedouins appeared before Tel Chai. The gates to the colony were closed. The siege began. For three days and three nights a handful of Jewish workers, men and women, defended themselves against over-whelming hordes of Arabs. The commander of the colony was Joseph Trumpeldor. Thanks to his military genius and to his courageous example, the colony lasted that long. On the fourth day the Druses sent an emissary who stated that the Arabs would withdraw from battle if the Jews allowed them to search the colony for French officers. Trumpeldor knew that there were only Jewish workers at Tel Chai, and he trusted the enemy. When he opened the doors of the colony, a troop of Arabs entered Tel Chai and began to shoot wildly. Too late Trumpeldor realized that he and his people had been the victims of a sly strategem. The killing began. The first woman to fall was Chanah Chizik. Trumpeldor decided to fight with his last drop of blood and to sell his life dearly. Shooting with his left arm, he and his surviving comrades tried to stem the heavily armed Arabian horde. But it was too late. Trumpeldor received a terrible shot in the abdomen. For a moment he had to stop shooting to gather in his intestines. He again gave the command and shot continuously until he could no longer stand. Then he died. His last words were — "It is good to die for my country."

Even at a time when Jews did not enjoy the privileges of equality they distinguished themselves by their bravery and their courage.

According to the report of the German Minister of War in the years 181 3 to 1815, 561 Jews volunteered for army service and 170 were raised in rank. One of the first soldiers decorated with the Iron Cross was a Jew by the name of Günsberg. Willibald Alexis describes a Jewish soldier in an article entitled "Mein Marsch Nach Frankreich" My March to France) in the Vossische Zeitung of May 5, 1899:

"The political questions of today remind me at this point of another comrade. He was a small dark unattractive man with nothing of the bearing of a gentleman. When he did not carry his gun, his weapons were scissors and needles . . . The fact that our uniforms still held together we owed to him. Whenever they showed any tendency to come apart, he was the first to prevent them from going back on their duty to their fatherland. Despite his unattractive appearance, he was highly respected. He was never involved in any of the petty quarrels that are unavoidable in barrack life. Everyone knew that he had conducted himself most bravely in previous campaigns and had been wounded several times. His name was Schwarsbraun, and he was Jewish."

In an article dated January 4, 1815 State Chancellor Prince von Hardenberg declared that:

"The history of our recent war against France has indeed indicated that the Jew remains faithful to the State that affords him protection. The young men of the Jewish faith were comrades in arms with their Christian fellow citizens, and we have found among them examples of true heroic courage and of glorious contempt for the dangers of war. Other Jewish citizens joined the Christians in every sacrifice."

In Austria, as in no other country in Europe, the Jews had an opportunity to participate in war service. Already in the 9th Century Jews stood by the Bohemians fighting against the heathens. In the year 1611 we find 500 Jews in the troops that defended the old and new city of Prague against the Passauer. Today in the Altneuschule of Prague there is a banner that Frederick III gave the Jews for their brave defense of Prague against the Swedish forces. When the Turkish War broke out in 1790, as well as in the following wars against Napoleon and the Wars of Liberation, Jews were found always among the ranks of the armies. In a list of the Austrian army of the year 1855 there were two Jewish majors, Simon Prisker and Ignatz Weiss, five cavalry officers, five captains, fourteen first-lieutenants and thirty-three lieutenants. In the Italian campaign of 1859 Theodore Jerusalem received the Order of Leopold, the rank of captain and of nobility because he had saved the flag of his regiment in crossing over the Lombro.

In his biography which was recently published in Budapest,

Otto Zarek, the German dramatist and novelist, devotes some reference to the Jewish war combatants:

'General Klapki stated, 'one-twelfth of our corp consisted of Jews. In all the battalions there were troops of Jewish volunteers. They fought bravely and with distinction. Many of them fell on the field of honor; a large percentage was advanced to officers. Many of the Jewish officers were decorated for exceptional bravery on the battle-field. Such an officer was Captain Aronyi who treed his commander, Count Leimingen, from captivity at Cibakhaza by boldly attacking the enemy. .. . The entire army and especially those men who fought at the front appreciated the courage of these Jews.

But what has Hitler to say about the Jews? That they "lack an idealistic state of mind" and that the "will to self-sacrifice in the Jewish people does not transcend a sheer drive for self-preservation."

How inane are these allegations of Hitler when we consider the heroic behavior of the Jews in ancient Palestine, in the defense of their belief during the Middle Ages and on all fronts during the World War. Is there any explanation for this hiatus between Hitler's contentions and the truth? Yes, there is an explanation that Hitler himself makes in "Mein Kampf," page 200. It is:

"The task of propaganda is not to weigh the rights of each side ... it does not have to state the truth objectively insofar as it is favorable to the others .. ."

CHAPTER 9

Protocols of the Learned Elders Of Zion

In maligning the Jews, the Nazis make particular use of the Protocols of the Learned Elders of Zion. Regarding the Protocols, Hitler states in "Mein Kampf":

"That the entire existence of the Jews is based on a continuous lies is best-revealed in the Protocols of the Learned Elders of: Zion, which they do so hate. 'They are nothing but a forgery- groans the Frankfurter Zeitung to the world. That is the best proof that they are authentic. What many Jews would unconsciously like to do is consciously exposed here ... It is quite immaterial from what Jewish mind these disclosures originate. What is significant is that they reveal with true exactitude the essence and the activity of the Jewish people and present their relations to one another as well as their final goals.

"The best critique of them is reality. Whoever studies the historical development of the last century from the point of view of this book, will soon understand the reason for the outcry of the Jewish press; for when this book becomes the common property of the people, the Jewish danger will be as good as gone."

These Protocols were indispensable to the Nazi campaign against Jewry. Every meeting held before Hitler's seizure of power was predicated upon the Protocols' alleged exposure of Jewish infamy. Numerous volumes have been written about the authenticity of the Protocols. When simple persons read them and believe them to be true, they become anti-Semites. Thus indoctrinated, their next step is to espouse Naziism.

The text of the Protocols from beginning to end is nothing but a mess of lies and forgeries.

Any reflective individual who reads the Protocols will see at first glance that they are criminal fantasies of the worst order, and that the Jews have had no possible connection with them. The Nazis cannot produce one iota of evidence that they are authentic. Unfortunately these very forgeries have led a great portion of the German people to hate the Jews, which is exactly what the Nazis desired.

The thundering voice of Hitler could not drown out the truth before a world tribunal. Here the false muddle of the Protocols would be as clear as day. What would the world's judgment be? These are not white lies that harm no one. They are a death sentence to millions of people. This criminally fraudulent work helped the Nazis to attain power in Germany and to draw up the disgraceful laws by which thousands of innocent people have been thrown into concentration camps and prisons, despoiled of their belongings and treacherously murdered. These Protocols enabled the Nazis to take away the daily bread of thousands of Jews and plunge them into misery and deprivation. Not only the Frankfurter Zeitung "groans" that they are a rank forgery. The whole civilised world knows that. Just as the Nazis have lied about the Protocols, so have they lied about everything else. The entire structure of Nazidom is based on filth, on lies, on degradation. Misrepresentation is the key note of its philosophy.

I am going to review the history of the Protocols and their attendant phenomena, in order that my readers will realise the extent to which this crime has been carried.

In the latter half of the 19th Century certain elements in Jewish life aimed at the establishment of a homeland for the Jews in Palestine. In the last years of the previous century Dr. Theodore Herzl came upon a plan. He is the real founder of political Zionism. He describes his objectives in the "Jewish State" (Judenstaat). In this book Herzl pointed out that the Jewish State was a world necessity.

Herzl did not mean that the Jews should suddenly flee from their adopted countries but that they should emigrate gradually and with the consent of the nations involved. The movement was to be fostered not only in compliance with the law but with the friendly cooperatiøn of various governments which would realise certain advantages from it. Herzl was accepted in the finest and most intellectual circles of Vienna and enjoyed great respect and popularity outside of the ranks of his profession. He was an editorial director of the Neue Freie Presse and was generally conceded to be a noble, generous and kind man and a helpful colleague. Anti-Semitism was obnoxious to him, not only because of the harm done to the Jews but because of the barbarity and intemperance it brought to European nations.

In 1897 Herzl and Max Nordau, an author, called a congress together at Basle. This Zionist Congress lasted three days. Its meetings were public. Aside from the delegates there were present, as is to be expected, many guests and journalists, among them many Gentiles. The delegates were made up essentially of middle class people, small merchants, small industrialists, attorneys, physicians and workers. Many of the latter were so poor, that friends or societies paid their expenses to the Congress. The language of the Congress was German.

It was later alleged by some criminal that the delegates to the Zionist Congress held in Basle in 1897 were called Free Masons and Elders of Zion and that in twenty-six secret sittings they conceived the diabolical plan of attaining Jewish world supremacy and dictatorship by foul means! To lend these lies a semblance of truth, the fabricated protocols of these would-be secret sittings were published in book form as the Protocols of the Learned Elders of Zion.

They appeared in the German language for the first time in the year 1919- Their translator and publisher was Gottfried zu Beek. In explaining the origin of the Protocols, Beek stated that they were read at secret sessions of the first Zionist Congress at Basle in 1897-

According to Beek, Czar Nicholas immediately had the Protocols translated into Russian. This translation was rendered by a certain Serge Nilus. Nilus tells how he came into possession of the Protocols: "All of this was taken by my correspondents from the secret archives of the Zionist Chancellery on French territory." Since Basle is certainly on Swiss and not on French territory, Nilus makes a liar out of Beek. He even contradicts himself. In the 1911 edition of the Protocols Nilus tells the following fairy tale: "The Protocols are a verbatim translation of the original documents, which a certain lady had stolen from one of the most important and influential leaders of the Free Masons after a secret session."

Thus the right hand of the forger was not aware of what the left hand did. Each translator of this forgery discredits the other. The publisher of the most recent German edition of the Protocols, Theodore Fritsch, reports the following in the preface to his translation: "In the year 1901 the Russian political police in a domiciliary visit to a Jewish home found a large manuscript in Hebrew, the translation of which was entrusted to Professor Nilus."

Which edition is correct—that of Beek, Nilus or Fritsch? Were the Protocols found in Russia, Basle or France? And when—in 1897 or in the year 1901? They are all fraudulent. They are all lies. Blinded by insane zeal and hatred, Beek, Nilus and Fritsch contradicted one another. They never suspected that some of their readers would verify dates and details.

When in Constantinople in 1921, Phillip Graves, correspondent for the London Times, became acquainted with a refugee Russian officer who offered him a badly frayed French book devoid of a title page, which the officer promised would be very interesting. Graves who wanted to help the poor fellow, bought the book. On reading it, he was amazed to find pages that he had read in the Protocols of the Learned Elders of Zion. Since the title page was missing, he did not know the author nor the name of the book. It later developed that this book was written by Maurice Joly, the title of which was "Dialogues in Hell between Machiavelli and Montesquieu", published in 1865- This work of the French attorney, Maurice Joly, was a veiled polemic against the administration of Napoleon III. The latters ambition had been to rule the world and make Paris its capitol. Such plans cost money, and since the French taxpayers were dissatisfied with them, the freedom of the press was restricted. Under these circumstances Joly did not dare to attack the policies of Napoleon III in the open but confined his remarks to a dialogue in the other world; even this eventually brought him a jail sentence.

Phillip Graves made a thorough comparative examination of the Protocol's and Joly 's book. He gradually came to the conclusion that the Protocols were nothing other than a plagiarism of the "Dialogues ", the only difference being that what Joly attributed to Machiavelli in the way of evil and lust for power, the Protocols attributed to the Jews. To expose this falsification the London Times ran three large articles by Graves on August 16, 17 and 18, 1921, which created a great sensation throughout the world.

These same Protocols were the cause of a trial that recently took place in Berne, Switzerland. Swiss National Socialists who had distributed the defamatory documents to foment anti-Semitism had to answer for their behavior in court. The court had called in a number of witnesses, all of whom exposed the Protocols as fakes. These testimonies were distastrous to the disseminators of such offensive literature.

A French Count declared before the court that the Protocols were a malicious forgery, while a Russian historian made a similar remark and produced evidence to substantiate his claim. M. Burzew, a world-famous Russian publicist, who had uncovered the sensational Asew case, voluntarily offered to testify in court in the interests of truth. All of these witnesses were Gentiles.

Chaim Weizmann, former President of the Zionist Organization of the World, testified that the protocols of the first Basle Zionist Congress were available in the Swiss National Library, and that anyone who would scan through them would realize that the so-called Protocols of the Learned Elders of Zion are nothing but a forgery speculating on the stupidity and vileness of man.

I should like to quote a few accounts of the trial from the Swiss press which was unanimous in its condemnation of the Protocols and those who distributed them.

"Der Bund" of Berne:

"When in 1921 the Protocols were exposed as a hoax, everyone felt that they would no longer be used as a basis for anti-Semitic propaganda. But everyone was doomed to disappointment. For they again emerged. Recently they have been used in Germany in the battle against the Jews and are also being read in Switzerland. Following a meeting of the National Front in Berne, these Protocols and other anti-Jewish writings were offered to the public by the National Socialists. The Jews are determined to defend themselves and above all want to expose these frauds to the world, even to Germany where such a trial could not take place and where the court would not dare admit the falsity of the Protocols."

"Luzerner Tageblatt":

"Dr. Weizmann clearly points out that whoever strives for world domination cannot be a Zionist, in other words, cannot work for a homeland for the Jews set apart from other nations, for the striving after world power, particularly in the sense of the alleged Protocols, would mean the opposite of isolation . . . This conviction is confirmed by other testimonies. The Protocols were the invention of the Russian Okrana, the secret police, who, signify cantly enough, had an office in Paris, since many Russians lived abroad. Ratschkowski is the name that is constantly mentioned; an obviously unscrupulous man who fabricated spurious documents according to his needs . . ."

The "Volksrecht" of Zurich on November I, 1934. ran a front page article entitled "The Forged Protocols":

"What has the trial revealed up to date? It has been established that in the year 1897 a Zionist Congress lasting three days took place in Basle. This was no secret congress as deluded Aryan nationalists and anti-Semites would believe. The Congress was open to the public. The protocols or proceedings of this Congress have long been in the Swiss National Library. Furthermore, a great number of Swiss Gentiles took part in the proceedings. Among them were the stenographers, Franz Sieber and Dr. Dietrich of Basle and also the journalist, Dr. Otto Zoller who attended the Congress as a representative of the Basle 'Nachrichten'. They are all still living. They appeared on the witness stand. They told the court what had occurred at the Zionist Congress. They testified man for man that the so-called Protocols of Zion, peddled about by the Nazis in Switzerland, are vile lies and falsifications from beginning to end . . . Two witnesses may be mentioned here, Professor Baumgarten of Basle and C. A. Loosli of Berne. Both witnesses stated that after careful investigation of the matter, they found that the Protocols were false, that they were fabricated in Russia and that their purpose was to incite pogroms against the Jews. Such pogroms have led to the most notorious and violent crimes in history.

"In recent persecutions of the Jews in Germany, these false Protocols have played a great role. Therefore we are happy today that the court has been spared the agitation of the Nazis and that these facts have been presented in a quiet manner and from an objective viewpoint. Disgrace and shame has fallen upon the Swiss Nazis, that they helped disseminate such a publication in Switzerland, a work that has been designated by German Gentile scholars and legal experts as offensive and trashy literature."

The experts in the Berne trial denied categorically that Zionist leaders ever desired a revolutionary policy or even political activity in the lands of the Jewish Diaspora. The entire Zionist movement is directed exclusively to Palestine. The official program of the proceedings of the Zionist Congress in 1897 was to create a homeland for the Jews in Palestine. One expert refuted the allegation of some anti-Semites that the author of the Protocols was Achad Ha' am, a Jewish writer and philosopher.

The actual protocols of the Congress, substantiated by the testimonies of those present at the Congress, indicate that all sessions were held in public. One expert stated that had such conferences really occurred, it would have been technically impossible to draw up the protocols within three days. There wasn't the slightest proof that any secret sessions took place in Basle during the three days of the Zionist Congress.

All of the basic material of the Protocols was taken verbatim from the "Dialogues", was elaborated and falsified in every respect. No less than 170 paragraphs were copied word for word. The falsification betrays the hand of an unconscientious, superficial plagiarist who did not take the slightest care to cover up all traces of a literary theft. Every where that Joly ascribes the dialogues of the dead to Napoleon III and his retinue, without mentioning them directly, the Protocols refer to world Jewry. We must regard it as a fait accompli that the Protocols in their final French translation under the direction of Ratschkowski, leader of the Russian secret police abroad, were completed in the year 1905 in

Paris and that later supplementary material was added. This forgery was used to convince the Czar that the Jews were responsible for Russia's bad situation because of their desire for world domination. The Czar was supposed to have believed that the Russian people were completely satisfied with the methods of his administration. Groups interested in the maintenance of absolutism thus attempted to prevent the Czar from introducing reforms that would have curtailed their power. The forger Ratschkowski was an evil spectre who did not hesitate to commit other forgeries and prevarications. The text of the Protocols later on was more extensively falsified by Serge Nilus.

Not one testimony upholding the Protocols as authentic could withstand serious examination. Above all, the witnesses constantly contradicted one another. Whenever the Nazis succeeded in finding an authority, on closer inspection he turned out to be a person of questionable moral value, if not a forger or criminal by profession.

The court also gave the defendants an opportunity to present their experts. It was a long time before they could find one.

It is an interesting and significant fact that the accused Swiss Nazis could find no Swiss expert. They had to find one who came from a country where anti-Semitism was, so to speak, bred by the State. This man who was to have established the authenticity of the Protocols had the name of Fleischhauer and came from Erfurt, Germany. Herr Fleischhauer made a long harangue before the Berne court. It lasted for days. What was the result? He succeeded in amusing the court. According to the unanimous reports of serious Swiss newspapers, Herr Fleischhauer succeeded in convincing neither the court nor anyone else of the authenticity of the Protocols. His inane remarks succeeded numerous times in producing peals of laughter. That was the extent of his success.

Since it is generally known that the Protocols are nothing other than a plagiarism of a pamphlet written by Maurice Joly, Fleischhauer suddenly made the discovery that Joly was of Jewish descent. As evidence thereof, he presented the presiding judge with a photograph of Joly and remarked that Joly resembled Karl Marx.

According to Fleischhauer, the editor of the Protocols was either Theodore Herzl or his contemporary opponent Achad Ha'Am, the Hebrew writer and philosopher. Fleischhauer maintained that the Protocols were completely edited and finished in Basle in the year 1897, thus simultaneously with the Zionist Congress.

All of these assertions were easily refuted. The brilliant figure of Herzl was known to every European. Everyone knew that this Zionist leader and idealist wanted nothing other than that the Jews should return to their own country. Achad Ha'am, on the other hand, was an advocate of cultural Zionism; he did not want to found a state for the Jews in Palestine but a cultural center to serve the Jewish spirit in the sense of the Bible and the Prophets.

The anti-Semites are characterized by their mendacity. First they swore that the Protocols were conceived in secret sessions of the Zionist Congress.

When it was established that no secret congressional sessions were held in 1897. other fables had to be invented. So they claimed that the Protocols appeared at the end of the last century, and that the trends of thought contained in them were the original work of the Jews. The fact that the Protocols were a plagiarism of Joly's book made them very unhappy for a long time until they conceived the brilliant idea of making a Jew out of Joly. Then they even went so far as to make Herzl or Achad Ha' am the author of the Protocols. Obviously they followed the principle that too many cooks do not spoil the broth.

Is it any wonder that these infamies, that these ridiculous paradoxes in Berne could awaken only laughter? Although usually very serious, the presiding judge could scarcely conceal his amusement. With contemptuous irony he would occasionally interrupt Herr Fleischhauer's torrent of words and inform him that the remarks of the "witness" were too presumptuous.

What C. A. Loosli said under oath at the close of the trial, deserves to be inscribed with golden letters in the history of civilisation. He maintained that all this tragic nonsense of anti-Semitism and Nordic supremacy was utterly devoid of truth. "If such murderers and sadists as Haarmann, Kürthen, Denke, Sternickel and Julius Streicher are of Nordic-Aryan descent and thus should be of nobler blood than our Jews in Switzerland," declared Loosli, "then I would like someone to take a well aimed shot at me, for I would not enjoy my earthly existence any longer."

On May 14, 1935 the verdict for which the entire civilised world waited was read. The chief defendant and former leader of the Society of National Socialist Confederates, Theodore Fischer, was fined fifty francs and five ninths of the court costs while defendant Silvio Schnell had to pay twenty francs fine and bear five eighteenths of the court costs. The essence of the verdict was that: (1) no proof had been established that the Protocols were authentic, (2) the finding of an original Hebrew manuscript of the Protocols is only an assumption, (3) that they are a plagiarism has been known since 1921.

Visibly aroused, the Judge shouted—"I feel shockingly repulsed at the thought of future dark ages, as have been prophesied here. I am no prophet but I wish to see a future in which one will be surprised to find that otherwise clever people had to break their heads for two weeks over the question as to whether the 'Zionistic Protocols' are genuine or forged. I deem the "Protocols'" to be a forgery, a plagiarism and silly nonsense."

That was the verdict of an impartial judge.

CHAPTER 10

Jews Look at You

A book entitled "Jews Look At You" recently made its appearance in Germany. Written by a certain Johann von Leers, it was dedicated to the notorious Governor of Franconia, Julius Streicher. The book comprises 95 pages and only six chapters. The titles of the chapters are briefly: (1) Bloody Jews; (2) Lying Jews; (3) Cheating Jews; (4) Degenerate Jews; (5) Artistic Jews; (6) Money Jews.

"Bloody Jews" treats of Jewish socialists. Among the "Lying Jews" are Professor Albert Einstein, Leon Feuchtwanger, the treacherously murdered journalist, Theodore Lessing, Theodore Wolff and Emil Ludwig. In "Cheating Jews", all Jews are designated as swindlers because of" the misdeeds of a few Jews. "Degenerate Jews" is devoted almost entirely to the famous sexologist, Dr. Magnus Hirschfeld. In "Artistic Jews", such talented artists as Max Reinhart, Elizabeth Bergner and Charles Chaplin are dragged through the mire. The essence of "Money Jews" is "that all Jews are blood suckers, money grubbers, millionaires and parasites." The book contains many photographs of Jewish artists, scholars and actors. These have been retouched and "corrected" to help convey to the German people the Nazi allegation that the Jewish race is the incarnation of all that is evil.

"Jews Look At You" is a play on the title of a popular children's book "Animals Look At You." In the latter the animals are depicted as lovable quadruped friends of man, while in the former the Jews are designated as hateful pariahs who are to blame for Germany's defeat in the War, for Germany's indigence, for the poisoning of the German soul, for everything that is wrong. The refrain is always the same hatred, infernal hatred! Over and over again the song of anti-Semitism is sung. Over and over again the vicious distortions rehashed. "Jews Look At You" was written and printed in a Hell. It is sold, disseminated and read in a Hell.

As an answer to this vile book, I shall present my readers with a list of Jews whose contributions to human progress and culture are of world renown.

These I, too, divide into six classifications. They are:

(1) Jewish Nobel Prize Winners.

(2) Famous Jewish Artists.

(3) Famous Jewish Physicians.

(4) Famous Jewish Writers.

(5) Famous Jewish Inventors.

(6) Famous Jewish Investigators and Explorers.

Whoever studies the Jews objectively, soon realizes that they are anything but inferior people. I cannot mention all the Jewish benefactors to mankind within these pages. I can, however, refer to a number of Jews who have liberated us from horrible diseases, who have raised our standard of living by their technical inventions and who have enriched our spiritual life by their music, their poetry, their novels and their philosophical works. Many undoubtedly will be known to my readers but not as Jews. How many people know that the inventor of the gramophone and of television was a Jew by the name of Berliner? How many know that Paul Ehrlich, who discovered neosalvarsan, a boon to the treatment of syphilis, was a Jew? How many know that Robert von Lieben, inventor of the radio tube, belonged to a people now designated as "inferior" in Germany? How many know that "Die Lorelei", one of the most popular folk songs in Germany, was written by Heinrich Heine, a Jew?

Heine was born on December 13, 1797 in Dusseldorf. He was the greatest German-Jewish poet. Heine loved Germany. In his "Nacht Gedanken" (Nocturnal Thoughts) he says: "When at night I think of Germany, my sleep is killed. I can no longer close my eyes, and my hot tears flow."

Characteristic of Heine was his tendency to grow sentimental in a lyric poem and to conceal his true feelings by concluding with ironic stanzas. Illustrative of this tendency is the following passage taken from "Winter Märchen Deutschland" (Winter Tales of Germany): "I wanted to cry where I once cried the bitterest tears. I believe that this absurd nostalgia is called love of fatherland. I do not willingly speak about that.

It is essentially a disease. I always hide my wounds with shamed mien from the public". In another part of the "Winter Marchen", he says—"and when I came to the border, I felt a heavy yearning in my breast. Even my eyes began to tear . . . and when I heard the German language, I felt something strange within me. I felt as if my heart were really bleeding."

In a letter he once remarked: "If I do not love my German fatherland more than all my Teutonic friends together, then I do not deserve to have my things read, sung and acclaimed in Germany, as is really the case."

Bismarck was a great admirer of Heine. He said on one occasion: "Had I been in his boots, I would have acted the same as he. Would I have been satisfied, if I had been born a Jew like Heine, to be shut up within the walls of the Ghetto at eight o'clock and be subjected to special restrictive laws? . . . These gentlemen forget that Heine was a Lieder poet, surpassed possibly only by Goethe. And they also forget that the Lied is a definitely German type of poetry."

In his "Ecce Homo" Friedrich Neitzsche says of Heine: "Heinrich Heine presented me with the finest concept of lyricism. I have sought in vain throughout the centuries for a sweeter and more passionate music . . . and how he treats the German language! It will some day be said that Heine and I were by far the first artists of the German language, vastly above everything that common Germans have made of it."

Friedrich Hebbel declared that: "Heine is a poet, a real poet, who does not dive into the sea for the pearls but rather lives below among the pearls and nixies and rules over their kingdom. All that we can gather from his appearance as well as from his speech." (Briefe, Tagebuch, Gedichte).

"... Heine's lyric poetry corresponds to the basic type of the German lyric and for this reason he is a German poet. . .." (1841. from the Hamburger Correspondent)

"... You have rendered Judith to me with greater profundity within one-half hour in Paris than all the German critics put together." (December 18, 1885, in a letter to Heine)

The literary historian, Wilhelm Scherer, was not blind to the essence of Heine's art. In his "Poetry of German literature", 15 edition, he says: . . and the names of Goethe and Heine will always be linked when reference is made to the German lyric. Heine belongs to our greatest lyric poets . . . for individual creative energy he deserves perhaps first place among the masters."

The great Danish poet, Hans Christian Anderson, on visiting Heine reported: "I heard only the throbbing of a German heart, the throbbing that is perceived eternally in his Lieder which are really alive." ("Story of My Life", page 140.)

Alexander Dumas (pére) mentioned of Heine: "France will accept the great poet with pride and with joy and count him among its own as soon as he but expresses the wish; unfortunately he loves Germany more than that land deserves." — Maria Embden'Heine, "Erinnerungen an

Heinrich Heine und Seine Familie" ("Memoirs of Heinrich Heine and His Family"), page 82.

Paul Ehrlich, inventor of neosalvarsan and Nobel Priz;e Winner, became famous as a young man through his discovery of the diazoreaction, a urine test, of great value to the diagnosis of typhus.

When at the beginning of his academic career he was forced to leave the University of Berlin because of his Jewish extraction, he set up his own private laboratory where he succeeded in proving that productive bodies were transferred from the mother's milk to the child. In the interests of science Ehrlich sacrificed not only a great portion of his personal means, which were far from considerable, but worked in the laboratory to the point of physical exhaustion. Let alone giving of his time and means, he actually jeopardised his own life by infecting himself with tubercle bacilli.

Ehrlich recovered, but the severe disease from which he suffered for a long time gave him the secret of immunity. This he discovered in the Institute for Serum Investigation in Berlin—Steglitz. Incidentally, Fransiska Speyer, a Jewess, donated a large sum of money to the Institute, which was very helpful to Ehrlich's studies. Along with Behring, Ehrlich was the founder of serotherapy. If what he had accomplished up to this time suffices to assure him immortality in the history of medicine, the discovery of neosalvarsan made him one of the greatest benefactors to humanity. This discovery, due to a combination of genius and unswerving perseverance, was made after 605 negative experiments. The 606th attempt succeeded, and thus a magic means arose to help free humanity from its direst scourge—syphilis.

For two years Ehrlich experimented with his new preparation on animals and collaborated with Dr. Hata, a Japanese physician. In 1908, along with Elias Metchnickoff, he won the Nobel Prize and finally the title of excellency from the German government. The last years of his life Ehrlich devoted to perfecting his neosalvarsan which at first was regarded with skepticism by cautious physicians and immediately declared worthless by nationalists, who considered it a Jewish invention. Today it is indispensable in the treatment of syphilis.

This great physician was possessed of an honesty and sense of honor that not even his enemies questioned. How many people he had helped secretly, only his private secretary knew. His attitude toward his subordinates is best characterized by the fact that they called him father.

Rarely did any man travel so wearisome and thorny a path to success as Albert Einstein, one of the greatest geniuses and physicists alive. When he was fifteen years old, his parents left Munich and settled in Italy. They gave up their German citizenship without acquiring other citizenship, a rashness that cost Albeit many years of deprivation. At sixteen years of age he took his entrance examination for the technical university at Zurich. He did very well in the mathematical sciences but failed in foreign languages. That was a bitter pill to him, particularly because his father had economic difficulties. Shortly afterwards Einstein passed the examination and became one of the outstanding students at the university. At twenty-two years of age he had finished all his examinations. He was prepared to earn a living but had to suffer for being a man without a country. Everywhere he was asked for citizenship papers, which he did not possess. He found no means of livelihood and became poverty striken. A gastric disease is his most vivid memory of this period of his life.

His friendship with other step-children of fortune, his absorption in the problems of physics and his passionate love for music helped him tide over these lean years. Despite want, he managed to scrape together enough money to apply for citizenship in Switzerland. In 1902 he was given a minor position in the Swiss Patent Office. For seven years he worked there as a technical expert. During this time he published his first great investigations. These aroused sensational interest, and his fame grew. In 1909 Einstein became examiner of patents in the Berne Patent Office and was appointed to the faculty of the University; in 1912 he was made assistant professor at Zurich and in 1914 was called to the University of Berlin. America was one of the first countries to recognize his genius. England, Holland and France offered him professorates. He received the Nobel Prize. On his lecture tours he was treated like a prince. In 1921 Einstein was given the honorary degree of Doctor of Science at Princeton University. Speaking in German, President Hibben of Princeton called Dr. Einstein the new Pythagoras who in the annals of science belongs in the same category with Pythagoras, Newton and Galileo.

After the World War Einstein was the first representative of German science to lecture in France. He spoke in the German language; nevertheless he was widely acclaimed throughout France. In Germany he received little recognition of his knowledge and perspicuity. As the educated laity became more interested in him, certain professional circles began to antagonize him — not because they understood or disagreed with his theory of relativity, but because he was a Jew. His chief antagonist was the "Collaborating Society of German Biologists for the Maintenance of Pure Science", a society that was never heard of before and has not been heard of since. Swastikas were sold at the doors of the lecture halls whenever Einstein spoke. Anti-Semitic colleagues contrasted him with "quiet German thinkers". Among these quiet German thinkers Paul Weyland mentioned Minkowski, a Jew. On his fiftieth birthday Einstein was to receive a small piece ofproperty from the city of Berlin. The grant was made public. On the following day the gift had to be returned, the Magistrate of the city suddenly having lost all legal rights to make such a disposal. The same thing happened to a second "gift" from the city of Berlin. Einstein knew in what direction the people ofpoets and thinkers was headed. He left Germany long before the National Socialist revolution and accepted gracious invitations to lecture in Brussels, Paris and throughout the United States. The indignities to which he had been subjected because of his Jewish descent only strengthened his tie with Jewry. He accepted Zionism and wanted it known wherever he went, that he was a Jew. The exceptional profundity of his theory of relativity and other theories has made it impossible for the public at large to realize the importance of Einstein. Notwithstanding he is the most popular physicist in the world.

The life of Emil Berliner reads like a sentimental novel with a happy ending. Berliner entered the world in Hanover, Germany, one of eleven children. His unhappy youth was replete with need and misery. At sixteen years of age he invented a weaving machine, which was not particularly original but the first indication of his genius. He spent some time at tedious jobs until 1870, when a great change took place in his life. A family acquaintance named Gotthelf, who had made his fortune in America, paid the Berliners a visit and took young Emil back to Washington with him.

Things were no better for him in America than in Europe. He did not like working in Gotthelfs store. He went to New York but did not want to settle there. After becoming a travelling salesman for a furniture firm in Milwaukee, he returned to New York where he found a position assisting Fahlberg, the discoverer of saccharine, in the laboratory. While he slaved at this position, he still possessed enougn energy to attend night school. A druggist friend, August Engel, gave him an old book on physics. He committed to memory the chapter on acoustics and electricity. Berliner lost himself in this book and soon made up his mind to become an inventor, in spite of the fact that he was earning only $10.00 a week, and experiments cost money. When he found a better position in Washington, he began his experiments in earnest.

Meanwhile the American inventor, Bell, in 1846 had constructed a telephone apparatus independently. Berliner was not acquainted with Bell's invention. He went his own way. After many disappointments, he was on the right track. His telephone apparatus consisted of a simple wooden soap-box to which an iron plate was nailed in lieu of a bottom. A cross bar was placed over the middle of the box. A common screw driven through the cross bar touched the center point of a metal sill. To the end of the screw a polished steel button was soldered, the button being the actual point of contact with the iron plate. Pressure variations were taken with the galvanometer. The entire construction of this small wooden box may be found with other relics of Berliner in the Smithsonian Institute in Washington.

On April 13, 1877 he sent his invention to the Patent Office. Because he had no money, he filed his own application for patent. After he received his next pay-check, he hired a patent attorney to complete the task. Since he could pay but little, the application was made out so erroneously that Berliner nearly lost all claims in later litigations. In 1878 he offered his patent to the Bell Telephone Company for $12,000, but his offer was refused. Later on, however, the Bell Telephone Company bought his invention for a moderate sum plus a good share in the profits of the Company.

As soon as he had the contract in his pocket, Berliner collapsed. Eight years of hard work and disappointments took their toll. But he gradually recuperated and carried on. The Bell Telephone Company showed a marked upward trend. In 1881 Berliner went to Europe and with his brothers founded the telephone factory of I. Berliner, which in due time became the center of the telephone system in Europe. The following years Berliner spent in research on the microphone and gramophone.

Berliner rendered great service in public hygiene, a field in no way connected with mechanics. At the turn of the century he discovered the deleterious effects of raw milk and demanded that milk be pasteurized. When he opened his campaign in Washington, the infant mortality rate in the first year of life was about 25%. Twenty years later, it fell to one-half that number. Through these measures the mortality incidence of typhus and paratyphus decreased considerably.

Berliner was a modest man, even when he became wealthy and famous. He gave generously wherever he believed he was acting in the interests of progress.

While most Jewish as well as non-Jewish inventors had to fight against dire poverty, Robert von Lieben was born into the world of brilliant and wealthy Viennese bankers and great industrialists. His only difficulty was that his father, Leopold von Lieben, wanted to make a cavalier out of him while he wanted to become an electrical engineer.

Robert was removed from the Gymnasium and entered the rigid secondary school (Realschule) only with great effort. He told his father that he did not want to take over the banking business but wanted to study physics. Despite his faulty preparation, young Lieben was sponsored and advanced at the University of Göttingen by the great physicist Nernst.

When he returned to Vienna later on, his father set him up in his own laboratory. The young investigator set to work at various technical problems and in 1903 published an article in a physics journal entitled "Investigations on Polarization of Roentgen and Cathode Rays".

In 1906 Lieben discovered that Cathode rays increase tone receptivity. This discovery first made possible the triumph of radio. It is well known today what the radio means to culture, to navigation, to aviation. The inventor of the amplification tube did not attain great material success. Lieben bore a malignant disease which killed him in 191 3 at the age of 3 5-

Hermann Aron, who was born in Kempen, Poland, entered the Cologne Gymnasium in Berlin at the age of sixteen and graduated at the age of twenty-two. It was with painstaking effort and private tutoring that he succeeded in advancing. He chose for his life's profession, and as his talent dictated, the breadless arts of mathematics and physics.

Yet he did not lose his interest in literature. In 1870 he delivered a lecture on Hamlet before the Heidelberg Academic Association, which produced a storm of applause and for a week was the talk of the University.

In those days the knowledge of electrical science, of amperes, volts, ohms and watts was theoretically known, but there was no definite way of measuring these units. Aron was the first to apply electrical current to the pendulum of a clock, and in this way a measure for electricity was established.

Aron also invented a rotatory current count as well as a differential spring which is an essential constituent of propelling vessels. Few people know that Aron was among the first pioneers in wireless telegraphy. He reported on such experiments at the International Electrical Exhibition in Vienna in 1883.

Aron left the industrial academy, where he had taught for two years, and became instructor in Physics at the Artillery School. He invented a gun recoil which in 1894 brought him the title of Privy Councillor. When he died in 1913, one of the outstanding pioneers in the field of electro-technology was lost to mankind.

Siegfried Markus, the inventor of the benzine automobile, was born in 1831 in Malchin, Mecklenburg, the son of a small business man. He had intended to become a craftsman, but because of the anti-Semitism he encountered, he could find no apprenticeship. Finally relatives in Hamburg apprenticed him to a Gentile master locksmith, who allowed the Jewish boy to live in a home where he could observe his religious dietary laws. After the conclusion of his apprenticeship in 1848, Markus came to Berlin and began to work for the firm of Siemens-Halske. His first invention was an improvement of the relay, a measure that increased the electrical energy of the reception station in telegraphy.

The Saxon administration bought this from him for $1,000. Markus did not like Berlin and went to work for Kraft, the court mechanic, in Vienna.

In 1860 he built a small workshop in his home in Maria Hilfer Strasse, 107- Here he constructed a benzine automobile that was ready for usage in 1868. He exhibited the model which aroused great interest. Most professional people were skeptical, and Markus found no one who would finance him. In 1875 he tried to drive the automobile through Maria Hilfer Strasse but alas, it would not go. The poor inventor was derided, and the police forbade further expeditions because of the ear-splitting noise. These adversities made Markus lose faith in his invention. With the help of a worker, he shoved the automobile back into the darkest corner of his shop and covered it with rags.

This expensive experiment cost him all his money. No one would lend him any more, because he was considered queer. Today the Markus automobile is one of the great attractions in Vienna's Museum of Industry.

A scientific explanation of the technical details of Markus' invention exists. In the official report of the 1873 World's Fair in Vienna, Professor I. E. Radinger wrote a thorough description of the principles upon which the automobile was built. Markus received a patent July 24, 1883 for an explosion motor. It was one of seventy-six patents that he had acquired from 1876 to 1898, among them was the first practical seismograph for the recording of earthquakes.

Markus died in 1898. Ten years after his death the Society of German Motorcar Industrialists wanted to place a memorial tablet in his honor on the wall of the house in which he was born. The largest automobile clubs of Austria and Germany, the firm of Siemens-Halske and the Society of Austrian Petrol Industrialists favored such a proposal. The owners of the house in Malchin, however, would not give their consent because they considered it unnecessary to honor a Jew. Considerable agitation arose in the press, but finally all efforts to honor Markus died out. Several years ago a monument was erected to his memory in Vienna.

Count Zeppelin is famous for his numerous experiments on airships. That he had a predecessor by the name of David Schwartz few people know. This Jewish lumber dealer was one of the first men to transfer theory to practice in the matter of air travel when he built his first motor and gondola. We may safely say that his airship was the first in the world.

David Schwartz, lived in Agram where he made improvements on wood-cutting machines, without any formal training in technology. He steeped himself in mechanics and soon realised that, like every thing else in the world, flying was also subject to the laws of mechanics. This thought became an obsession with him. He drew airships as best he could and figured out their size, their form and regulations. He believed that the balloon sheath had to be of metal, of very light metal such as aluminum. Working out plans to the finest details and calculating weights, gases and metals was a hard task for the lumber dealer. There was not a single person in Agram who knew anything about airship travel, and the few technically informed persons to whom he brought his plans discouraged him.

But Schwartz did not give up hope. When he had completed enough plans and blue-prints, he went to the Ministry of War in Vienna and presented his ideas. The Ministry was not receptive to them.

In Vienna he succeeded in interesting the military attache of the Russian Embassy in his project. After endless correspondence, Schwartz went to Russia. There he spent two years in painstaking experiments. When the aluminum ship was finished, the proper gas with which it was to be filled was not available. Conflicts arose with the Russian Ministry. When the time was up, and the airship did not fly, payment was suspended. After a few unpleasant experiences with the officers of the air corps, Schwartz; fled from Petersburg. He felt completely abandoned and betrayed. He destroyed the ship, demolished the motor, tore the supports and slashed the balloon. With a false passport he fled day and night, until he crossed the border. A lucky star led him to Westphalia where Karl Berg was working on aluminum. The latter saw a new field in the application of aluminum to airship sheaths. Years of aggravation, disappointments, deprivation and poverty followed. Finally the Prussian Ministry of War became interested in the undertaking and placed material and men at Schwartz's disposal.

When his dealings with Germany led to no results, new trips

and new efforts had to be made. He was tired of arguments with the officers of the air corps and with the factories which sent only useless motor equipment and inferior gas. An attempt to take off ended in chagrin. His hydrogen gas did not have the necessary lifting power. The chemical works at Atraszfurt could not set a date for the delivery of the necessary gas. There was no other source. The ascent was as uncertain as ever. Schwartz could no longer bear it in Berlin. He fled to Vienna. Here he awaited his fate. On January 13, 1897 the chemical works informed him that they were ready to deliver the necessary gas. A second telegram contained even more important news; he was summoned by the Prussian Ministry of War to appear for a test flight and was assured of acceptance and purchase. Great pleasure and satisfaction came to David Schwarts, but his poor heart, strained so long by many sorrows, could not stand the shock. He dropped dead from a heart attack.

The inventor was dead, but his work lived on.

The airship, the model of which can be found in the German Museum in Munich, was ready for flight, but no one would go up in it. A considerable sum had to be offered, before one of the subordinate officers by the name of Jagels would make the trip.

On November 30, 1897 the test flight was made. Despite very unfavorable weather (it was dreary and the wind blew at a velocity of from 7½ to 14 meter seconds) the airship rose to four hundred meters. Jagels was forced down. He descended so unexpectedly that the balloon was severely damaged. Nobody was hurt, but the Ministry of War considered the flight a failure, and that ended the fate of the Schwartz, airship.

In 1898 Schwartz's patent was sold to the Zepplin interests for I 5,000 marks. The importance of this Jewish predecessor was well recognised in Friedrich-shafen. Major Dr. Wileke, a friend of Count Zeppelin, once said of Schwartz;: "His work will go down forever in the history of airship travel."

Jewish Nobel Prize Winners

Facts and figures speak for themselves. Even the most vicious anti-Semite cannot question the facts and figures that I present here. There are 1,800,000,000 people in the world. The total number of Jews, 17,000,000, is less than one per cent of the total population of the world. There are 170 Nobel Prize-Winners in the world. Of these nineteen or twelve per cent are of Jewish descent.

In Germany there are 60,000,000 people, 550,000 of whom are Jews. Of thirty-four German Nobel Prize-Winners, eleven or thirty-three per cent are Jews. What does this mean? That one per cent of humanity has accomplished twelve times more than is expected from it, and that one per cent of the population of Germany has accomplished 33 1/3 per cent more than is expected from it. Yet Jews are persecuted throughout the world; particularly the German Jews, who have contributed a tremendous portion to the culture of their fatherland, are treated as second-class citizens and even worse. I ask you—isn't that stupidity? Isn't that an injustice that reeks to Heaven?

The Jewish Nobel Prize-Winners in Germany are: Paul Ehrlich (Medicine), Paul Heyse (Literature), Otto Wallach (Chemistry), Richard Willstätter (Chemistry), Fritz Haber (Chemistry), Albert Einstein (Physics), Otto Meierhof (Medicine), James Franck (Physics), Gustav Hertz (Chemistry), Otto Warburg (Medicine) and Adolf von Bayer (Chemistry).

Jewish Nobel Prize-Winners living outside of Germany but who belong to the German cultural sphere are: Alfred Fried (Peace), Robert Bárány (Medicine), Karl Land-steiner (Medicine), Tobias Asser (Peace).

Other Jewish Nobel Prize-Winners are: Gabriel Lippmann, France (Physics), Henri Bergson, France (Philosophy), Ilya Metchnikoff, Russia (Medicine).

Nineteen brilliant names on the firmament of human culture! Nineteen stars of eternal brilliance, nineteen geniuses! These Nobel Prize-Winners belong to a despised and persecuted race. They were chosen among one hundred and seventy of the most productive members of society.

Does Josef Goebbels know this? Yes. Does Alfred Rosenberg know this? Certainly. Do the other luminaries of National

Socialist Germany know this? Unquestionably. Yet they conduct a vicious anti-Semitic campaign and decry that the Jew is inferior. How unscrupulous they are, these leaders of Germany, who resort to Jew-baiting to attain their ends!

FAMOUS JEWISH ARTISTS

Mark Antokolski, born October 21, 1843 in Vilna, died in Homburg, July 14, 1902; most outstanding Russian sculptor of his day; lived in Paris since 1876; realistic monuments and works in Leningrad and Moscow.

Zachary Astruc, born 1835 in Angers, died in Paris 1907. French sculptor, painter, author and critic; friend of Edouard Manet who painted his portrait in 1864-

Max Band, born 1900 in Naumestis, Lithuania, painter. Lives in Paris since 1924: famous for his portraits of children.

Ludwig Barnay, born December 11,1842 in Budapest, died in Hanover January 30, 1924, actor; famous heroic roles (Shakespeare, Schiller); iounder of the German Theater Guild and of the Berliner Theater.

Leo S. Bakst, born 1868 in Grodno, died in Paris 1924, painter and graphic artist; particularly well-known for his colorful scenic paintings of the Russian Ballet.

Victor Barnowsky, born September 10, 1875 in Berlin; from 1905-1933 impresario and stage-director.

Sarah Bernhardt, born Rosalie Bernard in Paris September 25, 1844, died March 26, 1923, famous French tragedienne; since 1872 member of the Comedie Francaise, later directress of her own theater; specialized in the dramas of Victor Hugo and Sardou; also brilliantly portrayed the roles of Hamlet and Rostand's L'Aiglon.

Michael Beer, born August 19, 1800 in Berlin, died March 22, 1833 in Munich, a brother of Meyerbeer; dramatist; his one-act play "D. Paria," produced in 1823, received great applause from Goethe; his tragedy "Struensee" was produced on the stage through the efforts of King Ludwig I of Bavaria.

Leo Blech, born April 21, 1871 in Aachen, composer and since 1906 director in Berlin; 1923-1926 director of the State opera; his outstanding opera "Versiegelt" was produced in 1908.

Edward Bendemann, born December 3, 1811 in Berlin, died December 27, 1889 in Düsseldorf; next to Veit the most outstanding Jewish painter of the nineteenth century; from 1859-1867 director of the Düsseldorf Academy, Knight of the Pour-Le-Mérite; Works: the Sorrowing Jews in Babylon (in the Cologne Museum), Jeremiah (Berlin), and romantic compositions and frescoes in Dresden.

Charlotte Berend, born in 1880, painter and etcher of note.

Elizabeth Bergner, born August 22, 1899 in Vienna, actress; played Rosalind in "As You Like It", very successful in Berlin where she played Queen Christina, Viola and Saint Joan; since 1933 in London.

Otto Brahm, born Abrahamson 1856, died 1912, critic; director and impresario, pioneer-producer of Ibsen and Hauptmann, founder of the "Freie Bühne", wrote a biography of Kleist.

Alexander Cooper, 1605-1660, and Samuel Cooper, 1609-1672, world famous English miniature painters; the younger called a second Van Dyke by his contemporaries; miniatures of almost all members of the court and the aristocracy; several portraits of Cromwell.

Michele Costa, 1808-1884, composer and conductor in Naples; since 1829 in England, conductor of the Philharmonic Orchestra, of the Handel Festivals and of the Royal Opera; knighted in 1869.

Lorenzo Da Ponte, born Emanuele Conegliano 1749 in Venice, died in New York in 1838; wrote the libretto for Mozart's "Nozze di Figaro," "Don Giovanni," and "Cosi fan Tutte."

Ferdinand David, born in Hamburg June 19, 1810, died in Switzerland 1873, violin virtuoso, and pedagogue; since 1836 concert-meister of Leipzig Gewandhaus (world-famous auditorium).

Ernst Deutsch, born September 16, 1890 in Prague, actor; **1917 to 1933** in Berlin; one of the first exponents of dramatic expressionism.

Ludwig Dessoir, born Leopold Dessauer December 15, 1810 in Posen, died December 30, 1874 in Berlin, actor; famous Shakespearean character-actor at the Berliner Schauspielhaus.

PaulDukas, born October I, 1865 in Paris, important French composer; his symphonic poem, "The Sorcerer's Apprentice" (1897) is a favorite bravoura piece in Germany. Dukas died at the end of May, 193 5.

Mischa Elman, born January 21, 1891 in Talnoya, Ukraine, world-famous violin virtuoso; a brilliant technician.

Benno Elkan, born December 2, 1877 in Dortmund, sculptor; autodidact; one of the outstanding modern Jewish plastic artists in Germany; Works: war and cemetery monuments, busts and plaques.

Jabob Epstein, born November 10, 1880 in New York, sculptor; won fame for work in Paris and London; his extremely bold symbolic statues aroused much controversy in England.

Max Ettinger, born in Lemburg, December 27, 1874, composer; known for his songs and chamber-music and the operas "Juana," "Clavigo" and "Spring's Awakening."

Leo Fall, born February 2, 1873 in Olmütz, died in Vienna,

September 16, 1925, operetta composer, ranks with Lehar and Strauss; Works: "The Dollar Princess," 1907, "The Merry Peasant," and many others.

David Alexander Jeremiah Fiorino, born in Kassel May 3, 1797, died in Dresden June 22, 1847, most outstanding miniature artist in Germany; his numerous portraits characterized by charming and ingenuous delicacy.

Jean Gilbert, born Max Winterfeld February II, 1879 in Hamburg; composer of the popular operetta "Polnische Wirtschaft."

Karl Goldmark, born May 18, 1830 in Keszthely, Hungary, died in Vienna January 2, 191 5, composer; well-known for his opera "The Queen of Sheba", and his symphonies.

Isaac Grünewald, born in Stockholm September 2, 1889, painter; student of Henri Matisse in Paris; portrait-painter; one of the outstanding figures in modern European painting.

Jacques Halévy, born Elie Fromental in Paris May 27, 1799, died in Nice May 17, 1862, composer; among his numerous operas, the most famous "La Juive", 183 5. Halévy's nephew Ludovic Halévy 1834-1908 was Offenbach's librettist. Halévy's son-in-law was Georges Bizet.

Henrik Hertz, born Heymann in Copenhagen August 27, 1797, and died February 25, 1870, Danish dramatist and lyricist. His romantic dramas "Svend Dyring's House" and

"King Rene's Daughter" were frequently presented in Germany.

Ferdinand Hiller, born 1811 Frankfort-am-Main, died in Cologne 1885, composer, pianist and musical author; since 1850 director of the Cologne Conservatory of Music, where because of his influence, he was called the "Rhenish Musical Pope" by Richard Wagner.

Georg Hitzig, born in Berlin April 8, 1811, died October II, 1880, son of the criminal lawyer, Julius Edward Hitzig, architect; designed the Berlin Board of Trade Building, The Reichsbank, and the Technical University; Knight of Pour-Le-Merite; President of the Academy of Art, and Privy Councellor.

Juda Halevy, 1080-4145, poet and religious philosopher; classical representative of Hebrew poetry of the middle ages, lived in Cordoba, Spain and died on his way to Palestine. His most famous poem is the "Zionide", and "Elegie in Chaselen". His philosophical work, the book, "Kusari," was a depiction ofJudaism in the form of dialogues between a Jewish scholar and the king of the Chasares.

Bronislav Hubermann, born December 19, 1882, world-famous violin virtuoso; pedagogue and composer.

Oscar Kaufmann, born February 2, 1873, Germany, architect; designed many theaters in Berlin, among them the Volksbühne, Komödie and the interior of the Kroll Opera House.

Emerich Kálmán, born October 24, 1882 in Siópk, Hungary, operetta composer; most famous work was the "Czardas Princess", 1916.

Moise Kisling, born January 22, 1891 in Cracow, painter; since 1910 in Paris; at first a cubist, then a realist, particularly famous for his portraits.

Otto Klemperer, born May 15, 1885 in Breslau, conductor; 1927-33 at the Berlin State Opera House; exponent of modern music.

FritzKreisler, born February 2, 1875 in Vienna, world-famous violin virtuoso and interpreter of classical music; rendered great service to Germany, particularly during the inflation period.

Erich Wolfgang Korngold, born May 29, 1897 at Brünn, composed the "Snow-Man" at the age of ten; professor of Music in Vienna since 1927; his most famous opera "The Dead City," 1920.

Hermann Levy, born at Giessen November 7, 1839, died in Munich May 13, 1900, where since 1872, he was Court-Conductor; the first conductor of Parsival at Bayreuth in 1882.

Rudolph Levy, born July 15, 1875, renowned painter; lived in Paris from 1903-1914; neo-impressionist of the school of Henri Matisse; his landscapes, still-life and portraits are found in numerous German museums.

Ephraim Moses Lilien, born May 23, 1874 at Drohobycz, Galicia, lives in Badenweiler since July 1925, graphic artist; his sketches and etchings deal essentially with Jewish subjects, his outstanding works are his illustrations for "Juda" by Börries von Münchhausen and for "Songs of the Ghetto" by M. Rosenfeld.

Max Liebermann, born July 20, 1847 in Berlin, painter and graphic artist; trained in France, Holland and Munich, Germany; lives in Berlin since 1884- Began as a realist under the influence of Israel and later developed into the outstanding exponent of German impressionism; founder of the Berlin Secession in 1920; in 193 3 he was made president of the Prussian Academy of Arts; was dubbed Knight of Pour-le-Mérite; Honorary Citizen of Berlin; in 1927 President Von Hindenburg presented him with the Eagle-Shield of Germany. Liebermann was conscious of" his Judaism, and his entire artistic outlook was that of a typically Jewish artist, even in his North-German medium, and even though Jewish motifs rarely occur in his pictures. Liebermann died in 193 5 of a broken heart after the Nazis ousted him from his honorary positions and placed a ban on his works.

Pauline Lucca, born in Vienna April 25, 1841, died there February 28, 1908, world-famous singer; from 1861-71, she was the star of the Berlin Opera House ("Carmen," "L-Africana").

EduardMagnus, born in Berlin January 7, 1799, died August 8, 1872, painter; in 1844 professor at the Berlin Academy of Arts; outstanding representative of the school of Biedermeier.

He did portraits of Thorwaldsen, Mendelssohn-Bartholdy, Menzel, Rauch and many others.

Fritzi Massary, born in Vienna March 21, 1882, celebrated operetta-singer; Berlin 1904-3 3; married in 1918 to Max Pallenberg; indisputably the most outstanding representative of her profession.

GustavMahler, born in Kalischt, Bohemia July 7. 1860, died in Vienna May 18, 1911, composer and conductor; from 1897-1907 director of the Vienna Opera; the last of a series of great German symphonic composers; despite manifold romantic deviations from form he was tossed between naivete and sophistication, ecstasy and melancholy; a prototype of the Jewish musician. His most famous works are: "The Song of the Earth", 1911, ten symphonies and 42 songs.

Giacomo Meyerbeer, born Jacob Beer, Berlin September 5, 1791, died Paris May 2, 1864, opera-composer; lived in Paris from 1826-42, then moved to Berlin; was greatly opposed by Wagner whom he influenced in the beginning. "Robert the Devil" written in 183 I was a world-success. Other outstanding operas were the "Prophet", and "L-Africana". The Struensee Overture and his Torch-Dances are also well-known.

Erich Mendelsohn, born March 21, 1887 in Allenstein, architect, since 1914 in Berlin; 193 3 in London; is grouped among the leaders of modern architecture. His works are: the Einstein Tower at Potsdam, 1920, numerous business houses in Berlin, Nürnberg, Stuttgart, Chemnitz; Lodge of the Three Arch-Patriarchs in Tilsit; Jewish cemetery, Konigsberg, Edifices in Haifa, Tel Aviv.

Felix Mendelssohn-Bartholdy, born February 3, 1809 Hamburg, and died in Leipzig November 4, 1847, grandson of the philosopher Moses Mendelssohn; 183 5 conductor of the Leipzig Symphony Orchestra; 1843 founder of the Leipzig Conservatory of Music; resurrected Bach in 1829 by presenting the Matthias Passion; next to Schumann most famous composer of the German Romantic period; works prolific, among them, the oratorios, "Paulus" and "Elijah," many songs and piano selections and the famous "Midsummer Night's Dream" music.

Anton Raphael Mengs, 1728-1779; acquired great fame as painter to the courts of Saxony and Spain; Director of the Academy in Rome; considered by his contemporaries as the greatest painter of the epoch and reviver of classical art. Alfred Messel, born July 22, 185 3 Darmstadt, died Berlin March 4, 1909; architect; precursor of modern practical architecture; his Wertheim department-store building in Berlin (1904) and his museum in Darmstadt (1905) were pioneer works.

Amadeo Modigliani, born in Livorno July 12, 1884, died in Paris January 25, 1920, painter; since 1906 in Paris; exponent of expressionism.

Franz Molnár, born January 12, 1874 in Budapest; dramatist, whose comedies "The Devil," "The Game in the Castle" and many others have brought him world fame. His tragedy "Liliom" is rich in poetry (1912).

Siegfried Ochs, born in Frankfort-am-Main April 19, 1858, died in Berlin February 6, 1929; founder and master of the Berlin Philharmonic Choir (1882-1920) which he presented in the unabridged version of Bach's Matthias Passion.

Ignatz Moscheles, born May 30, 1794 in Prague, died in Leipzig March 10, 1870, pianist; teacher and composer; friend of Beethoven.

Jacques Offenbach, born June 20, 1819 in Cologne, died in Paris October 4,1880, operetta composer. In 1855 he opened the Bouffes-Parisiens; his world-famous success was "Orpheus in Hades"; his operettas and parodies were master-works of inexhaustable melody and creative genius; presented "Tales of Hoffman" in an entirely different light. Other works: "Beautiful Helen", "Pericles" and "The Bandits".

Max Oppenheimer, born July I, 1885 in Vienna, painter and graphic artist; expressionist; best known for his portraits.

Ernst Oppler, born September 19, 1867 in Hanover, died March I, 1929 in Berlin, painter and etcher; impressionist under the influence of Max Liebermann; his works: still life, landscapes and interiors are found in many German museums.

Moritz Daniel Oppenheim, born January 8, 1800 in Hanau, died in Frankfurtam-Main February 26, 1882, painter; famous for his paintings of Jewish family life and his characteristic portraits of Zunz, Heine, Börne, Riesser and Goethe.

Maria Orska, born March 16, 189 3 in Nikolaiev, Russia, died in Vienna May 15, 1930, actress; from 191 5 in Berlin where she excelled in roles from Strindberg and Wedekind.

Leonid Pasternak, born April 4, 1862, painter and graphic artist; from 1894 to 1921 Professor in the Moscow Art School; friend of Leo Tolstoy whom he often painted; Works: in Leningrad and Moscow; portraits of Adolf Harnack and Albert Einstein.

Max Pallenberg, born December 18, 1877 in Vienna, died in Carlsbad June **26, 1924,** actor; **1914 to 193 3** in Berlin; acted in melodramatic selections; played Moliere and other classics.

Camille Pissaro, born July 10, 1830, at St. Thomas, Virgin Islands, died in Paris Nov. 12, 1903, painter and graphic artist; descended from the Maranos; one of the precursors and masters of French Impressionism; his pictures and etchings, mostly landscapes, show no connection with Judaism.

David Popper, 1843-1913, outstanding violincello virtuoso in Vienna and Budapest.

Emil Pottner, born December 10, 1872 in Salzburg, painter, graphic artist and sculptor; best known for his animal figures; numerous porcelain images.

Max Pohl, born December 10, 1855 in Nikolsburg, actor; since 1884 in Berlin; from 1897 to 1932 at the Berlin Staats-theater. Famous for the roles of Shylock and Nathan.

Moriz Rosenthal, born December 18, 1862 in Lemberg, piano virtuoso of the greatest technical perfection. Student of Liszt.

Salomone Rossi, 1587-1628, the first outstanding Jewish composer; court conductor at Mantua; composed madrigals, cansonettas and instrumental sonatas. His "Cantici ebraici" written in 1622 are important liturgical compositions.

Karol Rathaus, born September 16, 1895 in Tarnopol, composer; outstanding in the field of modern chamber music; also wrote for the stage; his opera: "Alien Earth" played in the Berlin State Opera in 1930.

EmanuelReicher, born June 7. 1849 in Bochnia, Galicia, died in Berlin May 15, 1924, actor; in Berlin since 1887, famous for Ibsen and Hauptmann roles.

Max Reinhardt, born September 9, 1873 in Baden-bei-Wien, impressario and director; 1894 to 1902 was an actor under Brahm and then acted on his own; has produced: Wilde, Shaw, Maeterlinck, Hofmannsthal, Wedekind — famous for his productions of Shakespeare; his work indispensable to the history of the German theatre.

Sir William Rothenstein, born January 29, 1872 in Bradford, Yorkshire, famous English painter; especially well known for his portraiture.

Emmerich Robert, 1847-1899, actor; at the Burgtheater of Vienna since 1878; celebrated portrayor of heroic and lover roles.

Josef Rosenstock, born January 27, 1895 in Cracow, conductor; general music director in Darmstadt, Wiesbaden, New York and Mannheim; since 193 3 active in the Culture League of German Jews in Berlin.

Anton Rubenstein, born November 28, 1829 in Wechwotynez, Poland, died in Petrograd November 20, 1894, great piano virtuoso and productive composer. Chief among his works are the biblical operas "The Maccabees" and "Sulamith" and the oratorio "Moses".

Eugen Spiro, born April 18, 1874 in Breslau, artist; well known impressionist; lives in Paris.

Ernst Stern, born in Bucharest April I, 1876, graphic artist; as a scenic artist for years an associate of Max Reinhardt at the Berlin German Theatre.

Oskar Straus, born in Vienna April 6, 1870, operetta composer ranking with Lehar; outstanding work: "A Waltz; Dream" (1907).

Oskar Strnad, born October 26, 1879 in Vienna, architect; professor at the Vienna Art Industrial School; known for his stage designs.

Hermann Struck, born March 6, 1876 in Berlin, etcher and painter; since 1920 in Haifa; was one of the first artists in Germany to portray the Jewish element in paintings of Eastern Jewish types and Palestinian landscapes; excelled in graphic technique.

Adolf Ritter von Sonnenthal, born December 21, 1834 in Budapest, died April 4, 1909 in Prague, actor; since 1856 at the Vienna Burgtheater; director from 1887-1890; knighted in 1881; excelled in classical heroic roles.

RudolfSchildkraut, born April 27, 1862 in Constantinople, died in Hollywood July 15, 1930, actor; in Vienna, Hamburg and Berlin; since 1911 in America where he also played in the Yiddish theater.

Arthur Schnabel, born April 17, 1882 in Lipnik, one of the greatest pianists alive; famed interpreter of Beethoven; composer of abstract music.

Arnold Schönberg, born September 13, 1874 in Vienna, composer; from 1925 to 193 3 teacher at the Berlin Hochschule für Musik; exponent of the new or modern music.

JosefSchwarz, born in Riga in 1880, died in Berlin November 10, 1926, opera singer; famous baritone of the Bel Canto school, from 1915 to 1921 in Berlin; often in America.

Vera Schwarz, daughter of David Schwarz, opera singer.

Richard Tauber, born May 16, 1892 at Linz on the Danube, operatic tenor; since 1930 active in the movies and the stage.

Ernst Toch, born December 7, 1887 in Vienna, composer; leading in the field of chamber music.

Walter Trier, born June 25, 1890 in Prague, artist, etcher; renowned for his caricatures.

Bruno Walter, born September 5, 1876 in Berlin, world famous conductor; particularly well known for his interpretation of Mozart and Mahler.

Kurt Weill, born March 2, 1900 in Dessau, composer; his "Three Schilling Opera" a tremendous success; most popular exponent of modern music in Germany.

Egon Wellesz, born October 21, 1885 in Vienna, composer and music historian; student of Arnold Schönberg; leading exponent of modern music in Austria; ballets and chamber music; pioneer interpreter of Oriental music.

Jaromir Weinberger, born January 8, 1896 in Prague, composer; wrote "Schwanda" and "The Bag-Piper".

FAMOUS JEWISH PHYSICIANS

AlfredAdler, neurologist, born February 7, 1870 in Vienna; student of Freud; founder of Individual Psychology: Works: Practice and Theory of Individual Psychology.

Selmar Aschheim, born October 4, 1878 in Berlin; in 193 I made honorary professor of medicine; discovered the female sex hormone in the urine of pregnant women; pregnancy reaction.

Leopold Auerbach, 1828-1897, physician and biologist of note.

Moritz Benedikt, 1835-1920, neurologist, distinguished professor of medicine at Vienna; with Lombroso founder of criminal anthropology; pioneer in electro-therapy and diagnosis.

Julius Bernstein, 1839-1917. physiologist; professor at Halle; important work on muscular physiology.

Marcus Elieser Bloch, born in 1723 in Anspach, died in Karlsbad 1799, physician and pisciculturist; his fish collection now in the Berlin Zoological Museum. Works: "General Natural History of Fish," 12 volumes.

FerdinandBlumenthal, born in 1870 in Berlin, famous cancer investigator; 1905 to 193 3 professor at Berlin; now at Belgrade.

Gustav Jacob Born, 1851-1890, anatomist; professor at Breslau; together with Roux founder of developmental physiology.

Gustav Bucky, born September 3, 1880 in Leipzig; famous roentgenologist; since 193 3 at the University of New York.

Richard Cassirer, 1868-1925, psychiatrist, distinguished professor at Berlin.

Hermann Cohn, born in Breslau July 4, 18 30, died September 11, 1906, ophthalmologist; in 1874 he became distinguished professor at Breslau; founder of modern school hygiene; first to recognize the discovery of Robert Koch (tubercle bacilli).

Julius Cohnheim, born July 20, 1839 in Demmin-Leipzig, died August 15,1884, pathologist; professor at Kiel, Breslau, Leipzig; important anatomist; first to use histological freeze; Works: "General Pathology," 1878.

Wilhelm Fliess, born 1858 in Berlin, died in 1928; physician; famous for investigations and dissertations on the rhythm of life. Works: "The Course of Life," "On Life and Death."

Albert Fränkel, born March 10, 1848 in Frankfurt-an-der-Oder, died in Berlin, July 6, 1916, internist; professor at Berlin; in 1884 discovered the motivating agent of lung inflammation.

Sigmund Freud, born May 6, 1856 in Freiberg, Moravia, neurologist; professor in Vienna since 1902; discovered hysteria, neuroses, pathologic states of consciousness; founder of psychoanalysis; author of many works.

Ernst Friedberger, born May 17, 1875 in Giessen, died January 25, 1932 in Berlin, hygienist; in 1926 became director of the Dahlem Institute for Hygiene and Immunity Investigation; numerous studies in the field of hygiene.

Waldemar Haffkine, born 1868 in Priluki, Ukraine, died in Lausanne in 1934; talented bacteriologist; from 1895 to 1897 first to vaccinate with dead cultures against cholera and plague; from 1899 to 1905 head of the Haffkine Institute in Bombay.

RudolfHeidenhain, 1834-1897; professor of physiology and histology at Breslau. Studies on mechanical performance, warmth development in muscular activity and experimental testing of hypnotic phenomena.

Frans Jacob Henle, born July 30, 1809 in Fürth, died May 1 3, 1885, pathologist; one of the founders of modern scientific anatomy based on cellular findings; teacher of Robert Koch.

Jakob Herz, 1816-1871; since 1869 professor at the University and honorary citizen of Erlangen, which erected a statue in his honor.

Albert Hoffa, born May I, 1859 in Richmond, Africa, died in Cologne December 31, 1907, orthopedist; professor at Würzburg and Berlin; founder of modern orthopedia; special field: treatment of congenital hip dislocation; Works: "Manual of Orthopedic Surgery."

Merits Kaposi, 18 37-1902, dermatologist; student and successor of Hebra in Vienna; pioneer work in dermatology.

Georg Klemperer, born May 10, 1864 in Landsberg, famous physician; from 1919 to 1933 director of the Clinic of the University of Berlin; fundamental contributions to diseases of metabolism and nutrition.

Heinrich Kobner, born 1838 in Breslau, died in Berlin 1914, professor and occupant of the first chair in dermatology at Breslau; important works on skin diseases.

Hermann Küttner, 1870-1932, (Jewish descent, mother's maiden name Gerson), surgeon; professor at Breslau; navy staff physician; military physician in Greek-Turkish and World War; many works on war surgery.

KarlLandsteiner, born June 16, 1868 in Vienna, bacteriologist and serologist; member of the Rockefeller Institute for Medical Research; Nobel Prize for discovery of human blood groups, 1930; convert to Catholicism.

Richard Landsberger, bom December 23, 1864 in Darmstadt, founder of maxillary orthopedia (influence of the teeth on skull formation and organism).

Ludwig Lichtheim, 1845-1912, internist; professor at Königsberg 1888-1912; one of the founders of modern internal medicine.

Jacques Loeb, born April 7, 1859 in Mayen, died February 11, 1924 in Hamilton, Bermuda; German-American biologist; professor at the Rockefeller Institute; founded the doctrine of tropism.

Cesare Lombroso, born 1836 in Verona, died 1900 in Turin, famous Italian criminal anthropologist; professor of legal medicine and psychiatry at Turin; main exponent of the theory of born criminals; Works: "Genius and Insanity," 1864.

Otto Lubarsch, born 1860 and died 193 3 in Berlin, pathologist; professor at Berlin; important studies on tumors, metabolic pathology and immunity.

Alexander Marmorek, born 1865 in Mielnice, Galicia, died in Paris 1923, bacteriologist; superintendent of the Pasteur Institute; discovered the streptococcus serum; Zionist.

Otto Meyerhof, born April 12, 1884 in Hanover, physiologist, since 1929 Director of the Institute for Physiology at Heidelberg; did research on chemical processes and energy changes in muscular exercise; Nobel Prize, 1928.

IIja Metchnikoff,bom May 5, 1845 in Iwanowa, died in Paris July 15, 1916, Russian bacteriologist; professor at the Pasteur Institute; toxicologist.

Oskar Minkowski, born 1858 in Kovno, died in Wiesbaden 193 I, physician; Professor at Breslau; discovered relation between intestinal mucosa and sugar metabolism and thereby made possible the discovery of insulin.

Hermann Munk, 1839-1912, founder of brain physiology; professor at Berlin.

Ludwig Pick, born 1868 in Landsberg, pathologist; honorary professor at Berlin; founded pathological museums, female clinics and hospitals.

Adam Politzer, born 183 5 in Alberti, Hungary, died in Vienna 1920; professor of otolaryngology at Vienna; founder of modern otology.

Heinrich Poll, born 1877 in Berlin, anatomist; professor at Hamburg 1924-193 3; important studies in genetics.

Robert Remak, born July 26, 181 5 in Posen, died in Kissingen August 29, 1865; research on electro-diagnosis and therapy.

Mortiz Heinrich Romberg, born November II, 1795 in Meiningen, died in Berlin, June 16, 1873; professor of internal medicine; founder of pathologic physiology and neurology. His "Manual of Nervous Diseases" (1840-46) an outstanding work.

Ludwig Traube, born January 12, 1816 in Ratibor, died in Berlin April II, 1876, internist; professor of internal medicine; founder of experimental pathology; research in cardiac, pleural and renal diseases; introduced digitalis therapy of cardiac diseases.

Siegfried Tannhauser, born June 28, 1885 in Munich, internist; professor at Düsseldorf and Freiburg (1934); research on liver and gall.

Paul Gerson Unna, born September 8, 1850 in Hamburg, dermatologist; pioneer in histology; discovered the pathologic agent of the soft chancre with Ducrey.

Otto Heinrich Warburg, born October 8, 1883 in Freiburg, physiologist; chief of the Kaiser Wilhelm Institute for Cellular Investigation Berlin-Dahlem; discovered by his own method of gas analysis the metabolism of malignant tumors; Nobel Prize in 193 I.

Fernand Widal, born March 9, 1862 in Dellys, died in Paris January 14, 1929; professor of bacteriology and internal medicine; discovered with Gruber the Gruber-Widal reaction to typhus and paratyphus diagnosis.

Wilhelm Winternitz, born March I, 1834 in Josefstadt, Bohemia, died in Vienna February 22, 1917; founder of scientific hydrotherapy; 18814906 professor at Vienna.

Hermann von Zeissl, born 1817 in Vierzighuben, Moravia, died in Vienna 1814; famous Viennese physician; one of the most outstanding dermatologists of his time. Work: "Manual of Constitutional Syphilis."

Bernard Zondek, born 1891 in Wronke, gynecologist; 1926-193 3 professor at Berlin; director of the Hadassah Rothschild Hospital of Jerusalem; important work on the relation of the hypophysis to the ovaries; together with Aschheim founded the urine reaction for the diagnosis of pregnancy.

EmilZuckerkandl, born September I, 1849 in Raab, died in Vienna May 28, 1910, anatomist and anthropologist; professor and director of the Anatomic Institute of Vienna; studies on cephalometry; anthropological investigations.

FAMOUS JEWISH WRITERS

Peter Altenberg, 1859-1919 Vienna, prose stylist and poet; impressionist.

Sholom Asch, born January I, 1880 in Kutno, Poland; novelist and dramatist; honorary chairman of the Yiddish Pen Club;

Works: historical and modern Jewish novels— "Motke Gannew," "Three Cities," etc. Tragedies—"God of Revenge," "Sabbatai Zwi," etc.

Berthold Auerbach, born February 28, 1882, writer; opponent of Hebbel; outstanding works: "Village Tales of the Black Forest," "Biography of Spinoza."

Vicky Baum, born January 24, 1888 in Vienna; popular novelist and playwright; "Grand Hotel" her best known work.

Alice Berend, born 1878 in Berlin; wrote successful novels of bourgeois life.

Tristan Bernard, born September 7, 1866 in Besancon, humorous dramatist and novelist; popular in Germany.

Henri Bernstein, born 1876 in Paris, dramatist; his plays: "Israel," "Baccarat" and "The Thief."

Oscar Blumenthal, 1852-1917; successful musical comedy writer and critic; in 1882 founded the Lessing Theatre in Berlin.

Jean Richard Bloch, born 1884 in Paris, novelist of family life.

Ludwig Biro, born August 22, 1880 in Vienna; author of "Hotel Stadt Lemberg" and "Die Juden von Bazin."

Ludwig Borne, born May 6, 1786 in Frankfurt-am-Main, died in Paris February 12, 1837, brilliant journalist and political writer; one of the leaders of "Young Germany"; Works: Twenty volumes of "Collected Writings" 1825-1834-

Georg Brandes, born February 4, 1882 in Copenhagen, died February 19, 1927, critic; writer of exceptional influence; pathfinder for new talent from Nietzsche to Lagerlöf; Outstanding work: "Main Currents in the Literature of the Nineteenth Century."

Alexander Brody, 1863-1924, Hungarian writer; naturalist by profession.

Friedrich Dernburg, born October 3, 183 3 in Mainz, died in Berlin December 3, 1911, editor; brilliant stylist.

Alfred Doeblin, born August 10, 1878 in Stettin, writer and physician; novelist of note.

Ossip Dymow, born February 16, 1878 in Bialystok, Poland. Yiddish novelist living in America.

Edna Ferber, born August 15, 1887 in Kalamazoo, prominent American authoress, frequently portrays Jewish characters in her novels.

Leon Feuchtwanger, born July 7, 1884, in Munich, novelist; his outstanding works: "Power," "The Ugly Duchess" and "Josephus".

Bruno Frank, born June 13, 1887, in Stuttgart, dramatist and narrator; historical novels and stage selections.

Ludwig August Frankl, born February 3, 1810 in Chrast, Bohemia, died in Vienna March 12, 1894, poet; knighted (Ritter von Hochwart) in 1876.

Anatole France, 1844-1924, (Jewish grandmother), great French prose writer; famous for his participation in the Dreyfuss case.

Karl Emil Francos, born October 25, 1848 in Czortkow, Galicia, died in Berlin, January 28, 1904, novelist; deals particularly with Jewish themes.

Egon Friedell, born January 21, 1878 in Vienna, versatile writer; satires; historical themes.

Max J. Friedlander, born June 5, 1867 in Berlin, art historian and critic of world wide reputation; authority on old Flemish painting.

Ludwig Fulda, born July 15, 1862 in Frankfurt-am-Main, successful playwright and translator of the classics.

Heinrich Graetz, born October 31, 1817 at Xions, died in Munich September 7, 1891. Jewish historian; instructor in the Jewish Theological Seminary and professor at the University of Breslau; wrote the first intensive historical study of the Jews.

Maximilian Harden, born October 20, 1861 in Berlin, died in Switzerland October 30, 1927, critic and political writer; editor of many publications; essayist.

Heinrich Heine, born December 13, 1797 in Düsseldorf; died in Paris February 17, 1856, poet, essayist, satirist, lyricist, political journalist; noted for his ironic yet sentimental lyrics; most outstanding German-Jewish poet.

Georg Hermann, born October 7, 1871 in Berlin, novelist; devoted particularly to Jewish themes.

Theodore Herzl, born May 2, 1860 in Budapest, died July 3, 1904 in Edlach, founder of political Zionism; journalist and newspaper correspondent.

Moses Hess, born in Bonne 1812, died in Paris 1875, well known liberal political writer and precursor of Zionism.

Hugo von Hoffmannsthal, born in Vienna February I, 1874, died in Rodaun, May 27, 1929, great neo-Romantic poet; works: essays, poetic dramas and the texts to most of the operas of Richard Strauss.

Heinrich EduardJacob, born October 7, 1889 in Berlin, short story writer and novelist.

DavidKalisch, born August 23, 1820 in Breslau, died August 21, 1872 in Berlin, popular writer.

Karl Kraus, born April 28, 1874 in Gitschin, critic; polemical themes on speech, poetry and the drama.

Adolf L' Arronge, born March 8, 1838 in Hamburg, died in Switzerland, May 25, 1908, successful playwright; director of the German Theatre in Berlin.

Františék Langer, born March 3, 1888 in Prague, successful Czech dramatist.

Theodore Lessing, born 1872 in Hanover, philosopher and social writer; fought for equal rights for women, lor reforms in clothing, for peace and for understanding among nations; instructor in philosophy at the Technical University at Hanover; literary critic; murdered by the Nazis in Marienbad August 23, 1933.

Robert Linderer, born November 25, 1824 in Erfurt, died in Berlin Demember 16, 1886, librettist of German military music.

Emil Ludwig, born January 25, 1881 in Breslau, biographer of Goethe, Napoleon, Bismarck, Mussolini, etc.

Catulle Mendés, born May 22, 1841 in Bordeaux, died February 7, 1909 in Paris, novelist, poet and dramatist.

Alfred Mombert, born February 6, 1872 in Karlsruhe, poet; mystical lyricist.

Salomon Mosenthal, born January 14, 1821 in Kassel, died February 17, 1877 in Vienna, dramatist.

Max Nordau, born July 29, 1849 in Budapest, died January 22, 1923 in Paris, writer and physician; novels and dramas of historical nature; outstanding political Zionist.

Boris Pasternak, born February 10, 1890 in Moscow, poet, lyricist.

Leo Perutz, born November 2, 1886 in Prague; wrote fantastic novels and short stories.

Alfred Polgar, born October 17, 1875 in Vienna, critic and stylist; particularly interested in theatre criticism.

Josef Popper, born 1838 in Kolin, Bohemia, died 1921 in Vienna, social reformer and philosopher.

Marcel Proust, 1871-1922, famous French psychological novelist, (Jewish mother).

Roda Roda, born in Pusta Zdenci, Slavonia, humorist.

Carl Rössler, born May 25, 1864 in Vienna, humorist.

Joseph Roth, born September 2, 1894 in Schwadendorf, novelist; outstanding works "Job" and "The Radetzky March".

Felix Salten, born September 6, 1869 in Budapest, drama critic and short story writer; novel: "New People on Old Soil".

Moritz Gottlieb Saphir, born February 8, 1795 in Lovas Bereny, Hungary, died in Vienna September 5, 1858, journalist and humorist.

Antonio Silva, born 1705 in Rio de Janeiro, died in Lisbon in 1739, celebrated author of Portugese comedies.

Carl Sternheim, born April I, 1878 in Leipzig, dramatist; wrote many anti-bourgeois comedies; essays and stylized short stories.

Julius Stettenheim, born November 2, 18 3 I in Hamburg, died in Berlin October 30, 1916, well known humorist.

Heinrich Stieglitz, 180I-1849, poet; his life replete with tragedy.

Daniel Spitzer, born July 3, 183 5 in Vienna, died January II, 1893, feuilletonist of note.

Trimberg von Süszkind, 1250-1 300, the only known Jewish Minne-singer; six of his lyric maxims in Middle High German are preserved.

Arthur Schnitzler, born May 15, 1862 in Vienna, died October 21, 1931, leading German dramatist; novelist and short story writer.

Siegfried Trebitsch, born December 21, 1869 in Vienna, dramatist; translator of Bernard Shaw.

Jakob Wassermann, born March 10, 1873 in Fürth, died in Alt-Aussee January I, 1934, one of the greatest novelists in Germany; often treats of Jewish themes.

Semion Wengeroff, 185 5-1920, critic; outstanding Russian literary historian and lexicographer; author of numerous works on Russian Literature and its history.

Franz; Werfel, born September 19, 1890 in Prague, novelist; the greatest Jewish lyric prose writer of his generation; biographer; dramatist.

Hugo Zuckermann, born May 15, 1881, died December 23, 1914, poet; translator; Zionist.

Arnold Zweig, born November 10, 1887 in Glogau, dramatist, essayist and narrator of note.

Stefan Zweig, born November 28, 1881 in Vienna, famous novelist and dramatist.

FAMOUS JEWISH INVENTORS

Karl Arnstein, born 1887 in Prague, engineer; chief construction engineer at the Zeppelin Works; helped build the ZR III; lives in America.

Emil Berliner, born 1851 in Hanover, inventor of the microphone, telephone and gramophone.

Eugen Goldstein, born 1850 in Gleiwitz, died in Berlin in 193 3, physicist; discoverer of canal rays; introduced the name of cathode rays.

Oscar Matthias Eugen Liebreich, born February 14, 1839 in Königsberg, died July 2, 1908, pharmacologist; distinguished professor at Berlin; discovered the sleep inducing effect of chloral hydrate; introduced lanolin.

Robert von Lieben, born September 5, 1878 in Vienna, died February 20, 191 3, physicist; discovered the three-electron-tube which, once improved by Lee de Forest, made possible the radio and the talkie.

Siegfried Marcus, born 183 I in Malchin, died 1897 in Vienna, inventor of the benzine automobile and the telegraphic relay; member of the Academy of Sciences of Vienna.

Albert Neisser, born 1855 in Schweidnitz, died 1916 in Breslau, dermatologist; professor at Breslau; in 1879 discovered the gonococcus (pathothologic agent of gonorrhea); studies on leprosy and syphilis.

David Schwarz, born 1845 in Keszthely, died January 13, 1897 in Vienna, lumber dealer; invented the airship (first ascent, Berlin November 3, 1897); patent sold to the Zeppelin interests.

August von Wassermann, born February 21, 1866 in Bamberg, died in Berlin March 16, 1925, physician and bacteriologist;

since 1913 Director of the Kaiser Wilhelm Institute for Experimental Therapy and Biochemistry in Berlin; in 1906 he discovered the so-called Wassermann Reaction (blood test for syphilis) and achieved world fame.

Ludwig Lazarus Zamenhof, born December 15, 1859 in Bialystok, Poland; inventor of the international language, Esperanto.

FAMOUS JEWISH INVESTIGATORS AND EXPLORERS

Paul Ascherson, 1834-1913, botanist; Works: "Synopsis of Middle European Flora," "Flora of the Province of Brandenburg".

Emil Bessels, born 1847 in Heidelberg, died 1888 in Stuttgart, naturalist and polar explorer; in 1869 he proved the existence of the Gulf Stream eastward from Spitzbergen; in 1871 a member of the Hall Expedition on the Polaris; Works: "The American North Pole Expedition of 1879".

Franz; Boas, born July 9, 1858 in Minden, anthropologist; studies on North American Indians and Eskimos; professor at Columbia University, New York; outstanding work: "Culture and Race".

Hermann Burchardt, born November 18, 1857 in Berlin, explorer; undertook scientific expeditions in Syria, Persia,

East Africa, South America; killed by natives in South Arabia December **19, 1909-**

Emin Pasha, born (Isaak Eduard Schnitzer) March 28, 1840 in Oppeln, died in Kinema, Congo October 23, 1892, physician; naturalist in the Turkish and Egyptian Service; opponent of slavery; from 1890 tried to create a German Colonial Empire in Africa; killed by slave dealers. William II called him the "great son of his people".

Jakob Saphir, born 1822 in Oschmiany, Poland, died in Jerusalem 185 5, famous traveler throughout Asia, North Africa and Australia; itinerant reports on the Jewish Diaspora.

Eduard Glaser, born March 15, 185 5 in Deutsch-Rust, Bohemia, died in Munich May 7, 1908, archaeologist; conducted four expeditions to Southern Arabia.

Simon van Geldern, born 1720 Düsseldorf, died 1774 in Forbach, great uncle of Heinrich Heine, traveler of note; kept a Hebrew notebook of voyages throughout Europe, Africa and Asia.

Joseph Halevy, born December 15, 1827 in Adrianople, Turkey, died in Paris February 7, 1917, orientalist; professor at the Sorbonne.

Sven Hedin, born 1865 in Sweden (Jewish descent on mother's side), famous explorer; knighted in 1902; writer.

SiegfriedLanger, born 1857 in Schönwald, Moravia, explorer; killed on an expedition to Yemen in 1882.

Gottfried Merzbacher, born December 9, 1843 in Baiersdorf, died in Munich April 14, 1926, explorer; 1891-1908 in Persia, Arabia, India, Caucasus and Tien-Shan; a mountain in the Tien-Shan range called "Mt. Merzbacher".

MaxMoszkowski, born August 12, 1873 in Breslau, biologist and explorer in Sumatra and New Guinea.

RudolfSamoilowitsch, born September 13, 1881 in Asow, polar explorer; Krassin Expedition to rescue Nobile 1928; Arctic flight of the Zeppelin 193 I; Work: "S-O-S Arctis 1929".

CHAPTER II

Trial Balance of the Swastika

Until now I have merely refuted the accusations made against the Jews so that humanity might realise their mendacity. I do not play the role of a patroness of Jewry. Jews have rendered extraordinary services to humanity by their morality, their transmission of divine revelations and by their epochal inventions, research work and science. If despite this they still suffer persecution, torture and discrimination, it would hardly be possible for me, as a simple person, to afford them protection. I oppose anti-Semitism because I would otherwise be ashamed of my indifference, because I feel the deepest compassion for all victims of persecutions and because I am convinced that humanity can advance only by observing, weighing and judging matters without hatred or emotion.

Anti-Semitism is an attack upon the soul of man, hindering human progress. It is this attack that I wish to ward off and this insanity that I wish to banish from the minds of my contemporaries. I have proved that the Nazis assertion that the Jews are of an inferior race is clearly fraudulent. Jews are neither physically nor spiritually less valuable than other peoples.

I have presented evidence that the physical and spiritual differences between the Jews and the Germans are of no significance. The annals of history teach us that they are a courageous people imbued with boundless idealism. The Jews have given us our most beautiful and exalted moral laws. During the Middle Ages they showed the world what suffering and what tortures people with idealism can endure. Hardly had they emerged from the narrow confines of the ghettos before they began to work in the interests of humanity.

I have cited the achievements of the Jews in the fields of medicine, art and technology. I have indicated how Jews have liberated us from dreadful diseases and how they have altered the face of the universe by their technical accomplishments, especially the telephone, the automobile and the radio. I have told the story of Heine and of Ehrlich and have presented a long list of Jewish authors, artists, physicians, inventors and scientists who are the best proof that the assertions of the anti-Semites are only lies and calumnies. I have destroyed the fable of Jewish usury, swindling and cowardice. I have indicated that the Jews did not carry on any financial transactions until the twelfth century, and that after that time we Christians compelled them to exact interest, so that our sovereign masters could deprive them of it later. I have found that the Talmud proclaims and teaches the noblest of principles. I have quoted a long list of authentic Talmudic laws to convince my readers that they have been deliberately misinformed about the Jewish religion and particularly the Talmud by the Nazis. I feel that my fellow Christians who read this book, will abhor these incitors of hate who would impel them to anti-Semitic excesses.

As I have previously mentioned, we are not concerned with the protection of the Jews as much as with the protection of all mankind. There is no doubt that those people who defame their fellow men, because they temporarily possess the brutal power will themselves perish of this injustice. There is a God who will suffer no wrong. Remember the last Russian Czar who permitted pogroms against his Jewish subjects, so that innocent and defenseless people were slaughtered. For decades he humiliated the Jews just as Germany is doing today. Remember, how that Czar with his wife and children were shot without mercy in a dark cellar, and learn that violent deeds often find their retribution on this earth. We do not live forever. In the hour of death one's entire life is said to pass through one's mind. I cannot imagine how any one could leave this life peacefully and contentedly if he consciously had wronged his fellow-men. I do not even want to speak of the destiny which inescapably awaits men, according to the teachings of our religion, if during the years of their earthly life they have violated the most important commandments of our faith. Every anti-Semite is a sinner. He ought to know that our Lord detest nothing more than hypocrisy, than hate, than pitilessness, than the assumption of the role of moral judge when the judge himself is not free of guilt. How heavily all these errors must weigh in the scale of justice when throughout the centuries we have tormented and persecuted our fellow-men, when we humiliate and compel them to lead unnatural lives and then chide them about the wounds we ourselves have inflicted.

Whoever reads this book and still remains an anti-Semite, furnishes proof of non-belief in God. I go even a step further: I know that the majority of my Christian coreligionists reject anti-Semitism. That they are content merely to reject it makes them equally responsible for the agony of our Jewish fellowmen, for the horrible physical and spiritual suffering inflicted upon them merely because they are Jews. It is not sufficient to reject anti-Semitism. It is the duty of all good Christians to take an active part against it, and by spreading truth and knowledge, remove the disgrace of the Swastika. We must realize what dreadful injustice hatred against the Jews does to our children. In school and in their daily living they will be inclined to blame the Jews for any evil that may befall them. Hatred will prevent them from seeing things as they really are; it will obscure their judgement. For anti-Semitism as a mass expression warps the normal intellectual development of humanity.

Now I shall describe the German people under the Nazis, the crimes that have been committed in the two and a half years of National Socialism and the insanity of its rule.

Today there are less than 500,000 Jews in Ger many. They came to Germany in 321 A.D. as Roman citizens. There is historical evidence of Jewish settlements at that period in

Cologne, Treves and other parts of the Rhineland. The same is true of Augsburg and of Regensburg in Bavaria. The Jewish settlements perished during the great migrations. A new beginning was made under Charlemagne. In any event the Jews have lived in Germany for many centuries. During the Middle Ages and part of our modern times the Jews were segregated in ghettoes; they were barred from honest trade, and, therefore, could not contribute much to the welfare of their fatherland. Ever since they were liberated from the ghetto, they have rendered tremendous services to mankind in time of peace and war. 12,000 Jews sacrificed their lives for Germany during the World War. Let us recall once again the names of the great men in medicine and science and the great discoverers who have enhanced the glory of Germany throughout the world. I refer to the recipients of the Nobel Prize, who contributed greatly to the growth of Germany's fame. It is just these people whom the Nazis have treated most shamefully. They were declared by law to be second grade citizens of inferior race. The Nazi hooligans even discriminate against all persons who have any Jewish blood whatsoever. They resorted to the fraudulent term "Non-Aryan", to enable them to outlaw the Jews and other Germans of remote Jewish ancestry. It is self-evident that if a legislator designates a group as inferior, its neighbors, competitors and others will treat it as inferior. Germany has become a hell for the Jews who have to remain there.

The Nazis made many promises to their voters. They have kept none of them, save the promise to exterminate the Jews. This they have fulfilled. Many Jews have been murdered and many driven to suicide.

During a reception tendered him in London, the well-known author, Lion Feuchtwanger, related that he himself lost six personal friends in this manner. There is documentary evidence at hand that by the middle of June, 1933, 377 Jews were assassinated or driven to suicide in Germany. Only in one case was the perpetrator punished. He was an S. A. man from Würtemburg who was sent to jail for four days. Now they no longer kill the Jews, says Lion Feuchtwanger, they simply will not permit them to make a living. If a Jew decides to leave Germany, they plunder him and compel him to emigrate as a beggar. It is difficult to visualize what it means to live as a Jew in Germany of today. Feuchtwanger puts it thus: "I, for instance, love Germany. I was happy there. In Germany I realized the ideal of my labors. Now they have confiscated my house, destroyed my books, torn all my manuscripts, burnt scientific material which I had gathered, and annihilated the work of years. Even the flower beds in my garden were trampled upon. But I must confess, I still yearn for Germany's very air, landscape, people and language, for the serenity of my studies and the books in my library. And yet I could not return to Germany, even if its present satraps would guarantee the security of my life, my fortune and my library. For it must be like a nightmare for anyone who still has an understanding heart within him to live in a land that has become a terrible combination of a prison and a military training camp. Though one might be spared physical suffering, one is compelled to endure many humiliations hourly and daily."

The German author, Heinz; Liepman, has written a book entitled "Death-Made in Germany ". In the preface he states:

"I vouch by my honor, my existence and my life, that all events pictured in this book are founded on truth ... I left the land of my birth in-June, 193 3, the land for which my father fought as a volunteer in 1914, and for which he laid down his life on the battlefield in 1917 — I cannot sleep through any night, for I think of the Jews . . . Every night I hear a thousand moans, a thousand screams. I see eyes slowly dying, I see hands that have become bloody stumps and backs with skin distended like a balloon. I see bloody beards and broken bones, corpses, corpses! The Jews were not enemies. That is what robs me of my sleep. And they are being tortured and murdered even now, at the very moment I am writing these words. The sun shines and children are playing; men are breathing and flowers are blooming ... I know a Jew who was taken into a concentration camp, because a young attorney, his employee, coveted his practice and denounced him. Today this attorney has the practice while the rightful owner languishes in a concentration camp. When anyone addresses him, his face becomes distorted with fear, he cringes, and covers his head with his hands to protect it from blows. In his eyes there is a erased look. And because of this, because there are hundreds and thousands of such innocent men, tortured, despoiled and driven to insanity, I dedicate this book to the Jews murdered in Germany."

By special legislation a large number of attorneys, physicians and public officials, who could not prove that they had an Aryan grandmother, were thrown out of their professions. Even these Jews who were supposedly spared because they were front-line fighters during the War are being systematically boycotted . . . The Aryans who have not been openly identified with the barbarous Nazi regime and who would like to continue their normal business and social contacts with Jews are being terrorized by the S. A. and the S. S. and thus forced to avoid their Jewish friends. The majority of the German Jews have not enough money left to pay their rent, their gas and electric light bills. They must sell their household-effects for almost nothing. The Jewish children cannot attend school. Jewish youth can nowhere find work. In the smaller towns and villages where a few Jewish families have remained, they are subject to a permanent pogrom. Such Jews are forced to commit suicide.

In an article published in the "Journal of Nations", the well-known Italian politician, Carlo Sforza wrote: "One of my cousins spent the summer in a castle in Würtemberg. Because of her title she had the opportunity to visit some schools in which she was interested. In one of these she witnessed the following scene. During recess the pupils stood in line at the school kitchen where they were given a glass of milk and a slice of bread. When it was the turn of a little Jewish girl in line, the teacher called, 'Get away there, Jew. Next!'

"This scene was repeated daily. While there was no intention to give milk or bread to the Jewish children, no effort was made to spare them the torture of waiting in line. They had to stretch out their hands—that was demanded—but they had no right to food. The Christian children had to witness this scene day after day, so that they should learn how to treat a hungry Jewish child".

This was not written by a Jewish "atrocity propagandist" but by an Italian statesman.

Another incident is reported in the "Prager Presse". "Instruction in race theory is given in a certain school. The teacher wishes to demonstrate on a living model the typical characteristics of the 'Jewish Race'. For this purpose she commands a Jewish girl to stand in front of the class and asks the children to enumerate the various characteristics they discover. The girls mention a crooked nose, a round skull, black curly hair and thick lips. They can think of nothing else. The teacher asks: Is that all?' The pupils are silent. The teacher cries out: 'And how about the lying look?' Only after this torture is over may the trembling, scarlet faced Jewish child resume her seat."

A touching episode illustrating how the methods of the Third Reich react upon the individual was reported from Franconia. In Ansbach there was a Montessori school with Aryan and still a few non-Aryan pupils. One day after school was over the teacher left accompanied by a little ten-year old Jewish girl. As she came out of the schoolroom, she met an S.A. man in full uniform. He was the father of a pupil and had come to make some inquiries about her. When the little Jewish girl saw the S.A. man, she began to tremble, tore her hand away from her teacher and threw herself on her knees in front of the S.A. man. "I am a Jewess! Please don't do anything to me", she exclaimed, sobbing and shaking with fear. The S.A.

man stared at her stupefied, turned away and walked off with tears in his eyes.

A conference was held at the residence of Madame Anthony de Rothschild in London to consider the situation of the Jewish children in Germany. Stephan Zweig addressed the meeting, describing the hell in which the Jewish children of the Third Reich are placed. He cited the following examples:

A young girl wants to play with her companions. The other children avoid her and scream "Jewess" in her face. The Jewish child does not; understand what that implies but realises that she is a pariah among her former playmates.

A little boy sees his schoolmates wearing new brown uniforms. He asks his parents to buy such a uniform for him. The embarrassed parents attempt to explain that he, just he, is not permitted to wear such a uniform. The child does not understand why and feels insulted and humiliated. This is the humiliation, which the Jewish youth in Germany faces.

In the schools special rows of seats are designated for the use of Jewish children. Jewish pupils must endure silently and without protest the vilifications of their Aryan schoolmates. They may not attend places of amusement and are not permitted to participate in group excursions. Such places as beaches and swimming pools are barred to them. They are made to feel little by little that they belong to an inferior race.

The world famous woman fencer, Helene Mayer of Offenbach, has already been mentioned. Fraülein Mayer brought victory to the German flag at the 1928 Olympics in Amsterdam. At that time all of Germany applauded her skill. This charming young lady at fifteen was the champion of Germany and at seventeen had achieved world championship. In 1933 she suddenly discovered that she was no longer a German, that she belonged to the Jewish race and that she never again could represent Germany in any fencing meet. She emigrated to America where her activity as a master fencer is unhampered.

In the new song books used in the German schools there is a poem called "The Lorelei". There is an annotation to this poem to the effect that the author is unknown. Thus Heine's song is sung because it is euphonious and beautiful, but Heine is damned, because he was a Jew. Were he living today, he would have to write his poems in a concentration camp.

The great English Daily, the "Manchester Guardian", sent a special reporter to the Third Reich. He traveled the length and breadth of the country and then published his impressions. The English journalist describes the following occurrence which he witnessed. The house of an old Jew was besieged by a howling mob of National Socialists. The wife of the Jew is on her death-bed. The old man opens the door and pleads wtih the bestial crowd to let his wife die in peace. The mob jeers, and one zealous hero flings a big stone at the old man. Blood pouring from his head, he retreats into the house. Shortly thereafter his wife dies. After the funeral the old Jew leaves town. His life is not safe. He leaves all his wordly goods behind and grasps the beggar's staff.

Such Jewish beggars are plentiful in the Third Reich. That is the report of an English journalist.

The following letter recently was sent to me by a reader of my paper "Gerechtigkeit" (Justice). I reprint excerpts from it:

"Dearest Frau Harand ... At last I have recovered enough to write you a decent letter. Tuesday, they arrested me in the middle of the night. Seven men pulled me out of bed. Until three o'clock they kept me in a cellar, and then I was taken up to the second floor. There they hung some heavy weights on my feet, and for a full quarter of an hour six men beat me with rubber truncheons, whips and leather belts, until I was unconscious. When I regained consciousness, I was driven back into the cellar. Half an hour later I was taken out to be questioned. As I could make no more statements than before, the torture began, until I was again unconscious. I did not regain consciousness, until I was in the cellar once more. Blood was streaming from my nose, out of my ears and mouth. The worst of it was that my left forearm was broken. Still they beat me till I fainted. When I became conscious again, I was unable to rise. Then I received at least fifteen more blows with the rubber truncheon on my right shoulder. It is still impossible for me to raise my arm. I can hardly dress myself. But I would not talk. They told me that they would give me until six o'clock and would shoot me if I did not confess. Then they took me away. On the way out they showed me a corner in the yard where they intended to shoot me. In the darkness of the cellar stairs, they punched my face and kicked me from behind. Again I lost consciousness. At 8 o'clock they again dragged me out for questioning. 'This time they did not beat me. I was done for; I could not even think. They took me to a closed car. We drove to the police station. I could not get out, so one man kicked me out. They took me to a cell, but I collapsed in front of it. The prisoners carried me in, took off my clothes and applied cold compresses. Only today did they let me go home."

The world has heard a great deal about the concentration camps in Germany. The atrocities perpetrated there are so frightful, that I could scarcely believe it possible of human beings to commit such crimes. I did not intend to discuss these occurrences, but a few months ago my attention was called to a pamphlet in which Rabbi Max Abraham describes his own terrible experiences. He mentions names and vouches for the truth of his statements. Consequently I consider it my duty to publish some excerpts from this pamphlet. In the preface H. L. Reiner writes: "Here is another book among many about concentration camps. This one commands exceptional interest. While most of the disclosures about concentration camps heretofore were written by political opponents of the new government, this book informs the public for the first time of what happened to a Jewish clergyman. The most rabid opponent of Jewry can hardly consider it possible for a Jewish clergyman to sympathize with communism. It is the antithesis of his religion. All the more weighty, therefore, is the evidence which this Jewish rabbi here deposes about the martyrdom of men under 'protective arrest in concentration camps.

"Even the cause that brought him into the concentration camp is significant. He, a clergyman of a congregation near Berlin was accused of having attacked one of the S. A. leaders during anti-Semitic excesses on the night of June 26th. As a matter of fact, the Nazi had attacked the Rabbi and was slightly injured in the scuffle when his victim in warding off a blow, accidentally struck him.

"Here follows a devastating arraignment of the government. Not the young ruffian but the Rabbi was brought to the police station. There he first learnt the meaning of the new jurisdiction. He was beaten unmercifully by the S. A. and the S. S. while policemen stood by and watched.

"Then began his part of suffering through the German concentration camps.

"The terror did not begin in the concentration camp; in the police bureau another Jewish prisoner was forced to beat the clergyman with a rubber truncheon.

"This act of sadistic brutality was a proper introduction to Oranienburg. How much has been told about this camp, which is reputedly among the worst in Germany. And still the situation of these prisoners in 'protective custody[1], especially the Jewish ones, always astounds the reader. The Rabbi from Rathenow was the most important personage in the camp. Imagine what devilish pleasure the S. A. leaders derived from having this particular clergyman feel their whip.

"One cannot read the details of his treatment without asking whether these camp commanders and their underlings were human beings!" . . .

Every page of this document is replete with beatings, welts, starvation, shots, dark cells, infamous bunkers, murders and suicide; the record is a martyrology of our day. "It is a disgrace that Europe permits tens of thousands of men and women in Germany to be tortured in this inhumane manner and divested of their human dignity. This very indifference will some day bear witness against all of Europe."

Max Abraham had presentiments of things to come before the Hitler coup. He tried hard to counteract the dreadful prospect. In his pamphlet he states:

"In accord with the representatives of other religions, I tried to set a dam against the enmity to the Jews. One of my faithful allies was the parish priest who supported me courageously in my struggle. We had formed a working union for religious peace and harmony. Several times we delivered addresses together. The last time we spoke in December, 1932, at a meeting of the Tannenberg Club in Rathenow, both of us participated in a discussion of a hateful vilifier of both the Jewish and the Catholic religions."

It was all in vain. The revolution came and with it, sadism, concentration camps, inhumanity, lawlessness—all the things which stand for the Germany of today.

One chapter in Abraham's pamphlet is entitled "The High Holidays in the Camp". It reads as follows:

"The labor of cleaning out the latrines was the particular task of the Jews. It was especially ordered to be done on the Sabbath. 'Today is your shabbes again, you swine! Let us see where your God of vengeance is when we teach you flute tones in the pigsty'.

"The High Holidays were approaching. We asked ourselves fearfully whether the S. S. people were familiar with the dates thereof, because we dreaded worse torment. We, therefore, decided to make no mention of them. I, at first, had intended to ask the camp commander to excuse the company of Jews from labor on those days, but was finally persuaded by my comrades to desist as such a petition would not only be futile but might even have disastrous consequences.

"But we had forgotten about our relatives. They in their ignorance of true conditions in the camp had sent us congratulatory letters for the New Year. Since the letters had to be passed by the censor, the S. S. became aware of the dates and the secret was out. So I decided to go to the camp commander and ask for remission from work and for permission to hold religious services. The reply: 'Nothing like that permitted here'.

"The first holiday: At six o'clock in the morning we newly arrived Jews were called to a special summons. We were chased across the court yard in marching time. We were told to halt in front of a dungpit. Then we were ordered down into the pit and told to stand in line. I was torn from the midst of the company and placed in the center.

"The S. S. leader, Everling, roared at me: 'Now, Rabbi, you can hold your divine services here.' Everything within me resisted the order to literally drag our faith through the mire. I remained silent.

Everling: 'You refuse to comply with the command?'

'I cannot conduct services in a dungpit.'

"Everling pulled me out of the pit... rubber truncheons and the butts of guns rained upon me. I fell unconscious, and they dragged me into my bunk. For two hours I lay there unconscious. In the afternoon we were brought to the same dungpit where the others had to work all morning. Now Everling ordered me to give an address on Judaism and other religions. I began:

The Jewish religion like all others has ten commandments as

its foundation and also the beautiful biblical injunction: 'Love thy neighbor as thyself

"Everling interrupted me: 'Stop, you swine! We'll show you what we understand by love of neighbor.'

"Then I was so badly mistreated that I had high fever and convulsions. My body was so sore that I could neither sit nor lie down. Next day they transported me to the hospital, for I was in a precarious condition. Here I found myself among non-Jewish fellow-sufferers who cared for me. I will never forget their helpful kindness. When I fasted on the day of atonement, in spite of my weakened condition, they supplied me with food when the period of fasting was over.

"I stayed in the infirmary two weeks. Later I learnt that I was near death for several days."

Not only Jews had to endure these terrible tortures, but Catholics as well. A chapter in Abraham's stirring record is entitled: "The Catholic Cabinet Member in the Chamber of Horrors." It reads:

"On a Sunday in the middle of September, while I was still in the infirmary, a new 'protected-prisoner arrived with broom and scrubbing brush to clean the wards. It was the former member of the Prussian Cabinet, Welfare-Secretary Hirtsiefer, a well-known leader of the Centrist Party. He had been transferred that very morning from a concentration camp in Wurtemberg to Papenburg. Hirtsiefer gave the impression of an utterly distraught person. I had the opportunity to exchange a few words with him and tried to give him some courage.

"Next to our infirmary was the clothes closet. Each contingent of new prisoners was brought to this closet to be fitted for camp clothing. The prisoners had to disrobe completely for the fitting and were almost always dreadfully abused. What Room 16 was in Oranienburg, this clothes closet was here: a torture chamber full of medieval barbarities.

"Hirtsiefer was called into the closet. Soon we heard piercing screams. Since the closet was directly across from the infirmary, we could watch the whole process through the windows.

"We saw Hirtsiefer undress. He was a short stocky man. Several S. S. men surrounded him. They beat him unmercifully with rubber truncheons. We heard Everling scream at him: 'Have you said your prayers today yet, you swine? Have you seen the Pope yet? —did you rattle off your rosary? You have cheated millions of German compatriots as you were bidden by the Pope. Show us, you swine, how you pray with your rosary.'

"For refusing to pray before this pack of wolves, Hirtsiefer was continually beaten. Then came the fitting. To make Hirtsiefer ridiculous, they dressed him in half a trouser, a short coat, high boots and smeared his face with shoe blacking. Thus he was chased from station to station to present himself to his companions in misery.

"Not until late in the evening could Hirtsiefer retire to his bunk. He was completely exhausted. He scarcely had laid down, when a few S. S. men arrived. He was commanded to raise his arm in the Hitler salute. He obeyed. The men acted as though they had misunderstood the gesture and roared: 'What? You swine, you want to slap the S. S. men?' Hirtsiefer tried to defend himself—that he had raised his hand merely to salute as commanded. But the S. S. men hollered: 'No, you swine, you wanted to slap us.' And Hirtsiefer was thrown across his bunk and again brutally mistreated . . ."

After suffering martyrdom in various concentration camps and after a court trial which condemned him despite his complete innocence, to several months in the penitentiary, the clergyman succeeded in escaping to foreign parts. There he wrote his story, a document of humanity violated. This pamphlet should be read by everybody, even though it affords no pleasure. It should help to awaken Europe.

As can be learnt from Abraham's pamphlet, the atrocities in Germany are not limited to Jews. When the bestial elements in man are let loose they must find satisfaction somewhere. It may begin with Jews but soon spreads to their neighbors. Many Jews have been baptized in the course of the centuries. Many chose the Christian faith out of conviction and without compulsion. Many, however, were too weak to withstand the tortures and humiliations attendant upon loyalty to the faith of their fathers. It was natural for many men of Jewish descent to marry Christian women. Their children and grandchildren were completely assimilated among the Christian populace. This has happened all over the world. There are Christians in whose veins flows Jewish blood, and who are not even aware of this fact. Because the Nazis had to persecute the largest number possible, they attacked not only the full-blooded Jews but declared all Christians of Jewish descent to be outlaws. It is not jest but sad reality that there is an organization in Germany known as "The National Society of German-Christian Citizens of Non-Aryan or Not Purely Aryan Descent."

One of these Non-Aryans wrote to another, "I don't know whether you react the same as I do, but every one of the ugly jokes about the non-Aryan grandmother is like a slap in my face. That may be because I knew my grandmother well and loved her dearly. She was always a moving and stimulating influence in the family. I cannot believe that I received something dishonorable from the spurt of blood she gave me; nor can I grant to those who support this contention the right to pass judgment on such a blood mixture. My grandmother before her marriage bore a name which, though Jewish, occupies a very high place in the history of German art. I believe that the two families of noble Prussian lineage whose name and escutcheon I bear and who were quite beloved in our own province, never had any reason to be ashamed of this relationship, unless all concepts of decency, honor, order and diginity have been reversed in these last two years. I have two boys, dear comrade. They are ten and twelve years old. I am glad yet sad that I have them, because through them the fate of my beloved wife, to whose ancestral record no spying snooper could find any objection, is joined with mine. Were it not for the boys, I would not expect my wife for her own sake to further share my life. It is much harder to live now, for heretofore we shared it only with people of our own rank."

This is the letter of a non-Aryan. "In the new society every one constantly quotes his 'percentage'. Each believes himself better than his neighbor if he has 2½% more Aryan blood in his veins. The number of little groups grows daily. There are even 'Jews of pure race' but of the Christian faith in the society. They are differentiated as to whether they themselves, their fathers or grandfathers were baptized, whether they look like Jews or bear Jewish sounding names. The other extreme includes people who have invented the term 'not pure Aryan.' "The writer of this letter quotes a cousin who with pride and resignation 'takes 18¾% Jewish blood out walking every day!' He attends all the meetings in order to lord it over those who have a higher percentage and therefore are further removed from the sphere of Aryan sublimity than himself.

I mention these things only that my readers will understand to what degree this insanity of race is carried.

The people in Germany are not persecuted only because of descent but also because of faith. A Vatican publication reports that the Pope told three hundred representatives of German Catholic Youth organizations that he shares the pain and anxieties as well as the fear of German youth, that he receives news, unfavorable news, daily and that he is convinced that these young people demonstrate courage and faith reminiscent of the martyrs.

The Nazis attempt to excite the passions of the German populace by elevating the concept of "blood" to idolatry, by telling the Germans that they must consider themselves superior to all other peoples and that admixture of alien blood, particularly Jewish, will bring about the downfall of the German people. There are more than 20 million Catholics in Germany. In Catholicism blood or race play no part in the evaluation of man. It is apparent that this contrary conception would evoke controversy between the Nazis and the Catholic Church. Hitler's assertion that the Jewish race is inferior and abominable, is directly opposed to the attitude of the Catholic Church which holds that Jesus Christ, the Apostles and the early Christians were pure Jews.

The main attack upon the Catholic Church has been instigated by Alfred Rosenberg, who directs Hitler's foreign policy and who is his close friend. Rosenberg published a book entitled "The Myth of the Twentieth Century". Whoever reads this scurrility will at once recognize that there is absolutely no limit to the abuse and vilification that the Jews must tolerate in the Third Reich. My earlier chapters indicate what spurious accusations were levelled against the Jews in order to incite the people against them. I must confess, however, that the obscenities contained in Rosenberg's book overshadow all other lies told about the Jews in the course of history.

At this point I should like to quote a few of the lies Rosenberg tells about the Catholic Church and about Christianity as a whole, as reprinted in the "Monitor of the Cologne Archdiocese" of November, 1934- I have also taken my refutation of Rosenberg's allegations from this courageous paper.

Rosenberg writes:
"In Asia Minor the Romans ruled very strictly and collected taxes unremittingly; in consequence there arose in the suppressed populace the ardent hope for a leader and deliverer. That was the legend of Chrestos. From Asia Minor this Chrestos myth reached Palestine, where it was readily accepted, connected with the Jewish idea of a Messiah and finally transferred unto the personality of Jesus", (page 74-)

Of course, that is definitely a lie, because there never was a Chrestos legend in Asia Minor. About the Apostle Paul, Rosenberg has this to say:

"Inasmuch as the Pharisee Paul believed that the Christian revolutionary movement, by destroying the old living standards, would be promising and profitable for him, he joined it and went out preaching the international world revolution against the Roman Empire. His teachings constitute the Jewish foundation as well as the Talmudic-oriental side of the Roman Catholic and also the Lutheran Church . . . The Gospel of Saint John which still retains and breathes the spirit of an aristocracy, opposed this bastardization, orientalization and Jewification of Christianity." (pages 74-76.)

Let alone the other lies told by Rosenberg, we know that no political opportunism led Paul to Christianity. He was a disciple of Him who required that those who follow Him, take up his cross daily (St. Luke 9:23). After his conversion Paul really began to talk the road of the cross. In Damascus there was a plot to kill him, and he had to flee at night (Acts 9:23 to 25). In Jerusalem there was mistrust on the part of the Christians whom he formerly had persecuted (Acts 9:30). Then, prison, corporal punishment, danger from bandits, from heathens and from false brethren, exhausting journeys, night watches, perils at sea, worry about his daily bread, worries about the congregations, worries about individual Christians, who had become his brothers in the Lord, all these Paul experienced on the road of the cross, culminating in his martyr's death at Rome.

Rosenberg goes on to say that Christianity has adopted its customs and mores from an Asiatic people known as the Etruscans.

He says verbatim:

"With sadistic pleasure the Etruscans dwelled on all representations of torment, murder and sacrifice; human sacrifice was an especially beloved form of magic . . . This Asiatic people poisoned the Roman blood, and its ideas of hell's tortures and awakening terror in the hereafter were embodied in the Church; the dreadful animal-men-demons became and remained effective conversion media for the papacy. They pervaded the imagination of our Middle Ages already poisoned by the Roman Church, of which the art of painting gives frightening evidence ... Only when we recognise that this entire ideology is alien, when we become aware of its origins and are determined to rise up against it and rid ourselves of this monstrous spookery, only then will we have conquered the Middle Ages. And with it we will have destroyed forever the inner life of the Roman Church which is closely related to the Estruscan underworld tortures." (Pages 67-69.)

Scientific investigation has proven long since that Rosenberg adopted the fairy tale of the Etruscans and their influence upon Christianity from a certain Grünwedel, who in 1922 published a book entitled "Tusca". Gustav Herbig, a distinguished expert on Etruscan art and culture remarked before the Munich Academy of New Sciences in 1923: "I can say of him (Grünwedel) with perfectly good conscience exactly what he says of the Etruscan texts he claims to have deciphered—a product of insanity .. . idiotic sentences . . . genuine Etruscan infamies . . . vile jokes . . . untranslatable nonsense."

In this book Grünwedel, who formerly was held in high repute, seems to have fallen victim to hallucinations. He had been quite occupied with Indian cave paintings which impelled him to seek the guiding motive of Indo-Buddhistic art in pathologic sexual perversities and in the enigma of the Etruscan language, mythology and art. Out of pity for the author, the critics treated his book with silence.

Yet Rosenberg used this sullied material to spread the vilest lies and defamations against Christianity and the Catholic Church.

Rosenberg says of the Church in the Middle Ages:

"With an opportunity for unhampered self-development the nature worship of the Germans might have given way to a new ethical system of meta-physics and a new belief based on and guided by the concept of honor, had it not been for the interference of an armed Roman-Syrian Christianity. Alas, through Christianity other spiritual values entered and demanded first place, such values as love in terms of humility, mercy, submission and asceticism . . . Today every honest German clearly sees that this doctrine of love dealt a death blow to the soul of northern Europe . . . This medicine man, the Pope, as a demoniac figure cannot tolerate independent thinking any more than honorable acting on the part of his adherents. Quite logically, in order to fortify his position he tries to eliminate one as well as the other with all the means at his command. Toward that end he plays upon human fears and hysterical tendencies. He has to preach witchery and demoniac frenzy. By means of the Expurgatory Index, fire and the sword, he threatens all research leading to other findings and to liberation from the conception of the world as taught by himself". The medicine man throws a Roger Bacon into a dungeon as quickly as a Galileo. He declares a ban on the work of a Copernicus with the same ease that he tries to destroy all systems of thought that want to establish honor, duty and manly loyalty—in fact all teachings designed for personalities of high values —as life-giving potentialities."

That there were isolated popes in the Middle Ages who administered their office badly, no Catholic scholar will deny.

But to accuse all popes as Rosenberg does is baseness. And such distortion! Roger Bacon never was in a dungeon. Pope Clement IV was his protector and procured for him perfect freedom of work. Pope Nicolas IV who originally had compelled the scientist to live in the retirement of a monastery, restored his liberty to teach at Oxford, where Bacon, highly honored, died in 1294- Copernicus was the first to proclaim the principle that the earth revolves about the sun. Pope Paul III protected him and accepted the dedication of one of Copernicus' books. Even Galileo who enlarged upon the material of Copernicus was enthusiastically received by Pope Paul V and by Pope Urban VIII. It was only later that the works of Copernicus and Galileo were discarded when they were found to conflict with Holy Writ. In judging these matters, one must consider the period in which they occurred.

Christianity taught us Germans humility, love and compassion, a blessing to our people which we would never want to exchange for a doubtful conception of honor as extolled by Rosenberg. A true Christian has a different idea of honor than the Nazis.

On page 193 of his ***book*** Rosenberg states: "I cannot go into any more detail. Note only that the popes were paid a certain percentage by the whore-houses, from which Paul II (1464-1471) derived a constant revenue. Sixtus IV drew 20,000 gold ducats from the houses of prostitution. The priests had to pay certain taxes for their concubines, while the Vatican sent its officials to keep check on the bordello receipts. For a certain sum Sixtus IV even permitted pederasty."

I need not mention that all these allegations of Rosenberg are defamations of the worst sort totally devoid of any factual evidence. They remind one of the vicious lies told about the Talmud, and of the spurious Protocols of the Elders of Zion. Of the Old Testament Rosenberg says on page 603:

"Once and for all we must do away with the so-called Old Testament as a book of religion. We shall thereby thwart the attempt of the last millennium and a half to make us intellectually Jews, an attempt to which we owe among other things the present day material domination of the Jews."

On page 614: "... In place of the Old Testament panderer and cattle dealer stories will come the Nordic legends and fairy tales, first related quite simply and later accepted as symbols. The Nordic Germanic sagas will foster thoughts of honor and freedom and not those of murdering bestiality."

Whoever discards the Old Testament discards Christ. The Savior considered himself closely bound to the Old Testament. "Think not that I am come to destroy the law or the prophets: I am not come to destroy but to fulfill. For, verily, I say unto you, till heaven and earth pass, one jot or one tittle shall in no wise pass from the law, till all be fulfilled." (Matt. 5:1748.) To the rich youth Jesus said: "Keep the commandments." (Matt. 19:17-)

The Apostles also refer to the Old Testament. Their

preachments to the Jews culminate in the admonition, that in Jesus the prophecies of Holy Writ have found fulfillment. The gospels and epistles written by the Apostles and their followers are but one dissertation of this original sermon so closely tied to the Old Testament. Nor is it possible to construct a differentiation between the "Pharisee" Paul and the "Aristocrat" John, for all the Apostles, like their divine Teacher, were convinced that the writings of the old covenant were sacred writings. There are no less than 270 quotations from the Old Testament mentioned in the New Testament.

Just as the Church has its foundation in Jesus Christ, it is, like Christ, very close to the Old Testament in all its preaching and piety. It is not possible to relate in a few sentences how intimately strong, how alive and how fruitful this connection has been throughout nineteen centuries and will remain to the end of our days.

The Old Testament stands for the dignity of man, for honor and liberty and for equal evaluation of men regardless of station. The moral dignity of labor was first recognised by the Bible. Here laws of social justice were created and unjust enrichment and usury condemned.

In his Advent sermons, courageous Cardinal Faul-haber said: "Whoever will not acknowledge this inspiration and will not accept these books as the word of God and the revelation of God, will have to consider the people of Israel a super people. There is no other way. Either we believe in the inspiration of the sacred books or we must tell the Jewish people: 'You are the most ingenious race in the history of the world. "

Rosenberg also mocks at the New Testament, particularly the story of the Resurrection. Like some of his predecessors he dares make the assertion that Jesus Christ was not a Jew. The New Testament-testifies to the fact that Jesus was a Jew. "They are Israelites . . . from them comes the body of Jesus."

Is it any wonder that in view of the teachings of Rosenburg, twenty million German Catholics are being hindered from exercising their religion? The Nazis are in constant conflict with the Catholic Church. The Concordat reached between Germany and the Vatican is being violated every day.

The Nazis aim to control all the Germans, particularly the German children. Under their plan the children are to be educated without any religious training. The Catholic Church claims the right to educate its own children. That is the main reason for the conflict. Catholic youth organizations are per secuted, Catholic clergymen are arrested without reason and brought to the concentration camps. The highest dignitaries are prevented from publishing their sermons. Church publications are forbidden. Rosenberg, however, finds no word of criticism for his attitude toward a part of the German nation. He slanders the Church and everything we deem sacred. He expatiates and distorts the measures taken by the church government against infidels during the Middle Ages.

The Evangelical Church of Germany has a different struggle. The Swastika clearly indicates the direction toward which it is steering. The Nazis want to exterminate Christianity regardless of sect. They want to reintroduce paganism. They have no need for any God who condemns murder, theft and bearing of false witness and who requires love and mercy. These are obstacles in the way of securing power and exterminating their opponents. The Nazis aim to make heathens of the Germans. This they naturally cannot accomplish in a day. So they announce that full freedom of worship will be granted to all the people. But the state has provided that within the Evangelical Church there shall be a sect known as the "German Christians". This amounts to an attempt to convert the Evangelical Church into a servant of the state. At the the head of this church stands Reich Bishop Mueller, whose object is to incorporate Hitlerian dogma into the church and spread the idea that religion is only an integral part of the National Socialist Party and therefore must be subjected completely to the Party. As is well known, Luther wanted to restrict the power of the state. Hitler does not permit such restrictions. His demand is that religion shall put the power of the state above everything else. Even God must be put into the service of the state.

Honest believers resist Mueller. A majority of the Evangelical ministers and theologians has waged a stubborn war against this dissolution of religion. They demand freedom of worship. Pastor Hans Asmussen, in particular, has demonstrated unusual courage in his fight for the Confessional Church. "The church", he says, "must not be betrayed to the mundane power of the state". As a consequence to this struggle,

Evangelical clergymen are contimiously arrested and their religious services suppressed.

The pagans, however, are greatly in favor. There are several pagan movements. One group of pure pagans is led by Professors Bergmann, Wirth, Hauer Günther and Count von Reventlow. Then there is the Nordic movement of Dr. Rummer and the "Aryan Faith" of the wife of Field Marshall Luden-dorff. Dr. Mathilde Ludendorffs remark that the great poet Lessing was poisoned by the connivance of Moses Mendelsohn is indicative of her veracity. "Jehovah must know", she writes, "who provided Lessing with such large quantities of opium." Everyone knows that Lessing and Mendelsohn were intimate friends. Whoever is acquainted with Lessing's play "Nathan the Wise", and still spreads such lies, belongs in an insane asylum. Mme. Ludendorff makes Goethe the murderer of Schiller. She writes: "The lies exalting Goethe for a whole century obstructed the sacred blessing that arose from the murder of Schiller from coming to the German people. This blessing was that the people could learn about and acquire a ruthless racial hatred of the Jew, and thereby save itself" Rosenberg and Mathilde are lauded today, two people who by their lies make Germany utterly ridiculous and despicable in the eyes of the civilized world.

One of the hardest blows to the German people was the burning of the Reichstag. Today world opinion is unanimously agreed that the Reichstag was set on fire by the National Socialists as an excuse for exterminating their political opponents. Even the names of the Nazi incendiaries are known, their leader having been the infamous assassin, Lt. Heine. On the evening of February 28, 193 3, the Reichstag suddenly was engulfed in a blazing fire. The government immediately accused the Communists of arson, although there was not the slightest evidence that they committed this act. But the outside world soon discerned the fraud perpetrated by the Hitlerites. Ernst Torgler, the Chairman of the Communist faction, was arrested along with other innocent victims. In the trial that ensued, the treacherous crime of the Nazis against the entire German nation was exposed. Torgler and a few Bulgarian Communists had to be acquitted. Marinus van der Lubbe, a moronic tool of the Swastika, was executed. This base deception otherwise met with complete success.

From the very day of the fire the Nazis committed the most dastardly deeds of terror against their political adversaries. They immediately prohibited the publication of all Social-Democratic and Communistic newspapers and arrested all antagonistic political leaders. Thus their opponents could not campaign for the elections scheduled to take place early in March of 193 3- No wonder that the Nazis received so large an increase in votes that they could destroy all other German parties. The German Nationals and the Centrist Party had to yield. Whoever dared to object, was either incarcerated or murdered.

I do not want to enumerate all the crimes the Nazis have on their conscience. It was no accident when many of the assassins, who sped innocent people into the hereafter, were themselves slain by their murderous comrades. I need but mention June 30, 1934, the day on which Hitler had several hundred National Socialists ruthlessly executed. Among the victims were Gregor Strasser, Roehm, Ernst and Heine, all of whom belonged to the top command of the Nazi Party. Roehm was considered Hitler's best friend. Heine was implicated in the burning of the Reichstag and was a leader in the Party. He seemed to have apprehended his death, for he deposited a letter with a friend in which he admitted to have set fire to the Reichstag together with other National Socialists at the order of Goering. The friend was ordered to open the letter only in case Heine was killed by his comrades and then to publish it. In this way the last shred of doubt as to the guilt of the Nazis in burning the Reichstag was removed.

Which of his promises has Hitler kept? During his struggle for power he promised the working class Socialism. He promised higher wages and participation in factory management. What has happened to these promises today? The worker in present day Germany has absolutely nothing to say. The right to strike is absolutely forbidden him. The prices of foodstuffs and vital necessities have risen considerably, while wages have been reduced. Some wages amount to eight marks a week. Workers earning fifty marks a week and white collar employees who receive from 150 to 200 marks a month must tolerate deductions up to 3 3% of their wages. In addition employees frequently must make contributions and take subscriptions to various causes and pay entrance fees at demonstrations, all of which helps to further reduce limited incomes. All union have been smashed. The labor group in Germany is powerless to force any wage increases; its situation is unbearable. The unemployed are conscripted into the labor service or compelled to work on farms for almost nothing. The Nazis have dishonored their promises to labor. They have betrayed the workers as they have betrayed everyone else.

Hitler promised to eliminate the large department stores and the one-price stores which offered keen competition to the small tradesman and the artisan. But after he assumed power, the Nazis made a loan of fourteen million marks to the Tietz Department Store.

"The breaking of the slavery of interest" was another important point in the program of National Socialism. Interest remained unbroken. Those party comrades who dared remind the Leader of this promise were either shot or imprisoned. Gottfried Feder who was naive enough to take this point seriously and who as Secretary of the Interior demanded its realisation, was discarded. The same fate befell all of Hitler's old friends who dared insist that the social revolution follow the national one. Usurious interest is still collected in Germany. The only difference is that today the proportion of non-Jewish usurers is considerably greater.

National Socialism has always promised that all cartel agreements and trusts, like the banking and finance facilities, would be utilized for the benefit of the people. Whoever would dare suggest today that the great industrial institutions combined in agreements and trusts to maintain certain prices and which are gradually leading all the banks into the possession of the government, be so administered, would be a certain candidate for execution. The owners of the great factories, the powerful industrialists, are the real masters of Germany. They accumulate fabulous wealth, because their profits constitute the lion's share of the cost of re-arming Germany. While the people as a whole suffer great want, the big industrialists constantly become more powerful and richer.

What has Hitler done for Agriculture? The great landowners may be grateful for the repeated subsidies the Swastika awards them, but it is no secret that the peasantry is very dissatisfied with the law of entail, under which only the eldest can inherit the ground from his parents. The rest of the family is disinherited and must be content to find refuge with landed proprietors.

The Nazis have completely abrogated the right of free assembly and freedom of the press. It is out of the question for a group of citizens to hold a meeting if they intend to exercise any freedom of speech. Unless they are absolute adherents to the cause, workers, in particular, are not allowed to organize.

The same applies to employees, merchants, tradesmen or members of the professions. Only organizations founded to disseminate and glorify the principles of the Third Reich are permitted to exist.

The newspapers in Germany are utterly hopeless. They may contain nothing that is disagreeable to the government. Such newspapers as the "Berliner Tageblatt" and the "Vossische Zeitung", formerly read with avid interest the world over, are now the possessions of the National Socialists. They have sunk into complete oblivion. No one abroad considers them dependable reading matter. The once famous "Frankfurter Zeitung" is no different from the other newspapers controlled by the government. In the "Völkischer Beobachter", the personal organ of Hitler, such National Socialist leaders as Ley and Rosenberg publish all their vicious lies purposed to stupify, deceive and cheat the German people.

In this book I have offered my readers some evidence of the trends which are now the order of the day in Germany. Foul propaganda sheets run rampant. The "Völkischer Beobachter" is mild compared to publications that openly persecute Jews and Catholics. Such a publication is "Der Stumer"; its editor, the notorious Julius Streicher. Even decent National Socialists refuse to read this sheet, the contents of which can only emanate from a criminal or insane brain. Streicher knows no limitations. There is no obscenity or perversity that does not find room in this paper. And this Julius Streicher who castigates judges if they pass verdicts that do not please him, is the Chief Governor of Franconia and is cited to become the Police Commissioner of the city of Berlin. Hitler recently offered his heartiest congratulations to the publisher of "Der Stunner" on his fiftieth birthday.

No criticism of the measures taken by the government is tolerated. Any remark made privately or publicly means the dungeon or the executioner. In the last analysis all such restrictions and measures were taken by Hitler, Goering and Goebbels to build up the army. Rearmament is the paramount issue and everything else is secondary to it. For the "Reichswehr" has the decisive role in modern Germany. It is inconceivable that Hitler would undertake any move that would offend the army leaders. Naturally the National Socialistic hierarchy has no intention of doing anything against the army or the big industrialists. Nazi measures are directed only against the great masses of the people, against their free expression of opinion, against the Jews and Catholics, in fact against all real Christians. In such matters neither the army nor the industrial tycoons attempt to curb them. The Nazis attack Christianity because it stands for love of neighbor, mercy and justice, while National Socialism idealises only blood and race, glory and power.

Science has also been regimented. The elementary grades of the school system clearly bear the marks of the totalitarian teachings. Race theory and defensive sports have become the main constituents of the curriculum. Teachers are compelled to instruct history on the premise that its inception was from the north rather than from the Mediterranean. It is imperative that the students be taught that all cultures originated in Northern Europe. Nothing is to be presented objectively.

The universities were purged. Hundreds of professors, luminaries of the sciences, who founded Germany's academic fame, were driven out. Professor Herman Jacobsohn, dismissed from the University of Marburg, committed suicide under the wheels of a railroad train. The universally famous physicist, Albert Einstein, author of the theory of relativity, had to leave Germany forever. His scientific works were burnt on a pyre in front of Berlin University amid the applause of the National Socialists. Einstein was a recipient of the Nobel prize and the first German university professor to lecture in German in Paris after the War. Professor Franck, also a recipient of a Nobel Prize and a savant of world reputation, resigned "voluntarily".

The renowned physicist Born met with the same fate. Such famous mathematicians as Courant, Bernstein and Emilie Noether were ousted. The mathematics faculty of Berlin University was deprived of its most distinguished instructors. Among those dismissed from the Technical College was Professor Arthur Korn, a physicist, who developed the first practical methods of telescopy. Fritz; Haber, Nobel Prize winner and main exponent of a new school of chemists, discovered a means of obtaining nitrogen from the air. His name is symbolic of the highest development of modern German chemistry. The London Times of May 4, 193 3, in an article on Haber, stated that it is an irony of history that the Germans compelled a man to resign to whom more than anyone else they owe the fact that Germany had sustained the war for four years.

Germany has lost some of her greatest physicians. To such a man as Bernard Zondek, who was designated by the Swedish physician von Euler, a Nobel Prize winner, as the outstanding authority in his metier, we owe the discovery of the only accurate early diagnosis of pregnancy. The great scientist Friedman whose research resulted in the discovery of an important means of therapy for tuberculosis was dismissed along with his famous colleague Moritz Borchardt.

But they were not content with the dismissal of professors. The Nazi student body consigned the masterpieces of authors opposed to them to the flames. The works of the following were thus sacrificed: Max Brod, Alfred Doeblin, Ilya Ehrenburg, Lion Feuchtwanger, Jaroslav Hasek, Walter Hasen clever, Arthur Holitscher, Heinrich Eduard Jakob, Josef Kalenikov, Gina Kaus, Egon Erwin Kisch, Heinz; Liepmann, Heinrich Mann, Klaus Mann, Robert Neumann, Ernst Ottwald, Erich Maria Remarque, Ludwig Renn, Alfred Schirockauer, Arthur Schnitzler, Richard Beer Hoffmann, Ernst Toller, Arnold Zweig, Stefan Zweig and Adrienne Thomas.

One cannot help but ask whether any literary talent is left in Germany when such famous writers are proscribed. As a matter of fact a short time ago the Schiller prize was to be awarded, but the committee of judges declared that there was not a single poet in Germany who possessed the qualities that would entitle him to the prize. This does not matter to the students. The important thing to them is that dueling has been restored and they can slash at and cripple one another.

The following were excluded from the Academy of Poets: Alfred Doeblin, Thomas Mann, Jakob Wassermann, Franz; Werfel, Renee Schikele, Bruno Frank, Fritz; von Unruh, Georg Kaiser, Ludwig Fulda, Bernard Kellermann, Alfred Monbert and Rudolf Pantwitz. Max Liebermann, who for twelve years had been president of the Prussian Academy of Arts, the founder of the secession movement, a world famous artist, died of a broken heart, because the German government had forbidden him to paint.

The Nazi-inspired poets have no literary merit. Their protagonist is Hans Johst who formerly raved about the revolution. He is the only National Socialist author who deserves as high as second class rating. All others are quite insignificant. Hans Heinz; Ewers, who wrote the biography of the National Socialistic "hero" Horst Wessel, can be given some mention as an author. Ewers has undergone a change of mind since Hitler came to power. In 1922 he wrote the preface to Israel Zangwill's "Voice of Jerusalem" in which he expressed himself as very sympathetic to the Jews. Now, of course, Ewers is a follower of the Swastika. It is interesting to note that two books by Ewers, "Alruna" and "The Vampire", were both put on the Nazi black list of obscene literature.

Even music has been regimented in the Third Reich. Otto Klemperer, the director of the Berlin State Opera, and an excellent conductor, was dismissed from his post. Bruno Walter, orchestra leader of world renown, had to leave Germany. His place was filled by an unknown Herr Fuhsel. The general director of music at the Dresden Opera was literally dragged off the stage while conducting an opera. The most celebrated German pianist, Arthur Schnabel, leader of the master class for piano at the Berlin Conservatory of Music, was ousted. With him went the following: Emil Feuermann, the only German cellist of rank, Leonid Kreuzer, a fine pianist and teacher of the master class, Karl Flesch, famous violin pedagogue, Oskar Fried, Fritz Stiedry and Gustav Brecher, conductors of note and Bruno Eisner, the pianist. Hardly any of the German composers have remained with the Nazis. They ejected Arnold Schoenberg who wielded the greatest and most important influence on the development of modern music and who invented a new and unique musical language. Kurt Weill, the well known composer of the "Dreigroschen-Oper", had to leave Germany because he is a Jew. Franz Schrecker, an opera composer, was dismissed because of his not altogether pure pedigree. The proletarian composer, Hans Eisler, had to flee Germany. Thanks to the Nazis, German music has been despoiled of its most creative elements.

When the most famous conductor in the world, Arturo Toscanini, was invited to direct the Bayreuth Music Festival during the Richard Wagner Memorial year, he sent the following telegram to Mme.

Winifred Wagner as a protest to the treatment of his German colleagues by the Nazis:

"Since the events which have offended my feelings as an artist and a human being have not changed despite my hopes, I consider it my duty now to break the silence I have kept for two months and to notify you that it is better for my peace of mind as well as for yours and everyone else concerned not to consider my coming to Bayreuth any longer. With the friendliest feelings for the House of Wagner.

—Arturo Toscanini."

Many talented actors have disappeared from the great German Theatre. Fritz; Kortner, Max fallenberg, Mesdames Messary and Bergner and the world famous directors, Max Reinhart and Jessner, were driven out of Germany. Lotte Schoene, Frieda Leider and Alexander Kipnis cannot sing there any more. Käthe Kollwitz, the great artist, had to flee the Reich. The best known film directors emigrated from Germany.

The Nazis also conquered the radio and used it as an instrument of propaganda. All programs are made to conform. The unfortunate radio listeners in Germany have to endure the eternal brass music of nationalism and eternal fiery harangues.

A lady whose veracity is not to be doubted told me after her return from Germany what has happened to the intellectual circles there. These people told her plainly, "the only right we still possess is to degenerate. We do not know what is going on in the world." People, who think, no longer read newspapers because they despise the stupid nonsense that is being disseminated. When Goering was married, column after column in the newspapers was devoted to the wedding ceremony, the ladies' gowns, the presents and the bridal gift. One woman writer told me that people angrily tore up these papers.

Most intelligent people in Germany are opposed to the Nazis, but feel powerless to do anything. There is the case of a lady who adopted a seven year old boy. One day he came home from school and told her what a great hero Ludendorff was. When she said that General Ludendorff had been defeated in the war, and that he had managed to escape by wearing a disguise and dark glasses, the child stared at her unbelievingly. She could not tell him any more, or she would have endangered both their lives. The German children are being taught the greatest absurdities in the schools, but the parents dare not interfere. Everyone is afraid of spies. People do not want to make new acquaintances and are even suspicious of their friends. It is like the Tower of Babel. People no longer understand each other. They retire from public life. One lady took an Austrian visitor to the movie theatre. For two hours they saw Germany marching. For two hours they heard ecstatic Heils. Then enlarged close-ups of the leaders were shown. The head of Julius Streicher, bald and homely, appeared on the screen. Streicher screamed: "The most important thing to the people is race." The ladies could scarcely keep from laughing aloud. Hideous Julius Streicher speaks of race! Hitler, Goering and other prominent leaders were shown, but none seemed so ridiculous as this man Streicher, who measures up to the Nazi concept of beauty so miserably and yet has the temerity to bring up the race question. After the performance, the theatre was as quiet as the grave. Neither a word of commendation nor one of criticism.

In addition to spiritual sufferings there are other difficulties reminiscent of the war years. Germany's export business diminishes daily. Consequently there is a shortage of raw materials, especially textiles. In the first two months of 1933 Germany exported goods amounting to 812 million marks. In 1934 this export amounted to only 693 and in 1935 only 600 million marks.

In January and February of 1932 Germany's export surpassed the import by 112 million marks, while the first two months of 1934, the import was 57 million higher. In the first two months of 1935 the import was 162 million marks higher than the export. Goebbels has forbidden the newspapers to mention this drop in German export business. Germany must import enormous quantities of materials for armaments, and there is no limit to these imports. It is more essential to the Nazis that the Germans eat substitutes than that they produce less poison gas or fewer cannons. Dr. Schacht recently gave notice to the people that they soon will have to do without many commodities. Before long they will again revert to the card system of the war years. It is not even possible to find enough goods for all the flags that have become such an absolute necessity in the Third Reich. The materials people will not buy from Germany can be procured from England. The boycott waged against Germany by the entire world is not directed by Jews. Many important firms in different European countries and in America refuse to buy German goods, because they do not want to deal with a country ruled by such inhumane monsters. Naturally the Jewish merchants of America, Roumania, Poland, Lithuania, Holland and Czechoslovakia, who formerly bought great quantities of goods from Germany, will no longer buy there. Who can blame these people that they will have nothing to do with a country that persecutes their coreligionists so maliciously?

Germany's relations abroad are as bad as her internal relations. In conformity with Hitler's "My Struggle", the Nazis espouse the idea that only those of a superior race have the right to live and that the Germans are the most superior race in the universe. To provide room for this superior race of Germans, certain neighboring peoples must be destroyed and exterminated, so that the 250 million Germans expected in the next hundred years can find requisite space. These ideas have made Germany the most hated and isolated nation in the world. France sees in Germany her worst enemy. All assurances of Hitler and Goering do not change this attitude. France is preparing for war against Germany. Thanks to the Nazis, France has entered into a military alliance with the Soviet Union. All attempts by Germany to estrange England from France have failed. Undoubtedly in case of war, we would find England on the side of France. Czechoslovakia also has a military pact with Russia. Poland has made a ten-year pact of friendship with Germany, but in well-informed political circles it is rumored that in case of war, Poland will withdraw. Germany cannot count on Roumania or Hungary and certainly not on Austria for any assistance.

The way Hitler proceeded against Austria aroused the indignation of the entire civilized world. The Nazis are determined to annex Austria. As I have stated previously, the Austrians as a people have never yearned for anschluss with Germany. Some were greatly opposed to it. Only a few politicians prompted by selfish motives wanted to sacrifice Austria's independence. When the National Socialists found they could not persuade Austria to seek such a union voluntarily, they attempted to apply force. They began to organize violent brutalities against Austria.

In January, 1933 the Viennese police discovered a stock of explosives at the home of a Nazi partisan. From Germany came order to instigate constant disturbances in Austria. On July 11,1933, Dr. Steindle, leader of the Tyrolean Heimatschutz (Home Guard) was shot by Werner von Alvensleben, a citizen of Germany. In Vienna, a jeweler by the name of Futterweit was killed by a bomb. The Hak department store in Vienna was demolished on July 31, 1933 by a carefully planned explosion. Indeed, so carefully were all these bombs and explosions planned, having covered almost every part of the country, that in each case the perpetrators were provided with automobile transportation across the border to Germany by reliable party members.

When on July 19, 1933, a group of Christian Austrian athletes were attacked with hand grenades by two Nazis and one death and several injuries resulted, the National Socialist Party in Austria was prohibited from activity of any sort. The Storm Troops and "Schutzstaffeln" were dissolved, and the wearing of any party insignia was forbidden. Most of the Austrian Nazi leaders fled to Munich, which became the center for all operations against Austria. In August, 1933, the police discovered an information center in the office of a certain Dr. Schneider who was in regular contact with the foreign office in Berlin. Soon thereafter a news bureau in the office of Ludwig Stiegler, a civil engineer, was raided. Here information was steadily sent to Munich. At the end of September a similar news bureau was discovered in the rooms of an organization for the blind, the secretary of which was a German citizen. This led to the finding of important documents which proved conclusively that the Nazis had established a chain of information bureaus all over Austria. News was furnished from official offices, from industrial plants, banks and the professional organizations. The police, the army, organizations of a patriotic character, the volunteer militia factories and enterprises of all sorts were spied upon. The results of this espionage were written up as reports and sent to Munich where they were broadcast over the radio in a distorted form.

The bombings and terroristic acts of July, 1933 were followed by a marked increase in Nazi propaganda. The walls of houses, the trees, streets and rocks were painted with the swastika. Circulars and metal swastikas were distributed everywhere. In the country they lit swastika flares on the hills. On October

I, 193 3, tear gas attacks were launched against merchants, coffee houses and movie theatres. At the end of October, the first paper bombs exploded, followed regularly by more violent explosives. These paper bombs were smuggled into Austria from the German border. One of the largest of the smuggled shipments was held up at the border late in December, 193 3-

In addition to hundreds of thousands of circulars, newspapers, pamphlets and forged Austrian government manifestos, these shipments contained hand grenades with and without handles, some of which had been used during the last year of the war. Toward the end of January, 1934 the number of explosions increased daily and reached their peak early in February.

When the cohorts of the Swastika realized that the way to power in Austria was blocked, they started to try new methods. The Austrian Nazis proclaimed a series of strikes. Meanwhile Hitler decreed that every German citizen spending his vacation in Austria had to pay a tax of one thousand marks. At the same time the Nazis attempted to kill Austria's tourist trade by acts of violence and by explosions.

Just before Whitsuntide a number of explosions took place in railroad stations. Thereafter there were daily bomb attacks upon railroad property, electrical plants, water works, telephone wires, public buildings and residences. It was only too obvious that this terror was organized and directed from Germany. On June 9, 1934, sixty-eight pieces of explosives, packed in a sack from the Bavarian Salt Works, were found in Upper Austria. On June 11, 1934, a deposit of explosives was discovered in Telfs. At the end of May a whole succession of terroristic acts occurred in Salzburg Between June 10th and 12th many telegraph wires in Lower Austria were cut and the poles destroyed. In the Tyrol attacks were directed against several electrical plants and water works. Here, too, it was soon discovered that the German Government had a hand in these happenings. Vicious attacks were made daily on policemen and soldiers. A renegade Nazi, Kornelius Zimmer, who was suspected of having given secret information to the police, was murdered by his former comrades.

At the end of July the smuggling of weapons from Germany into Austria began in earnest. The Nazis were preparing for the grand "Putsch." After a few days of rest they set off several explosions in Klagenfurt, in front of the court house, the government building, the central office of the police department and in the courtyard of the rectory. These were the last sporadic explosions preceding July 25, 1934, on which day the swastika called upon its Austrian partisans to openly rebel, the first victim being Chancellor Dollfuss.

The following description clearly demonstrates that the death of the courageous chancellor was planned at official headquarters in Germany. The man who tenaciously and indefatigably defended Austria's liberty and independence wanted to drive out the plague of National Socialism at any cost.

Nazi leaders in Germany succeeded in interesting Dr. Rintelen, the ambitious Austrian ambassador to Rome and former Governor of Styria, in their plans. Several high officials of the Viennese police promised cooperation. It was planned to surprise the entire cabinet, which was scheduled to meet on July 24th, make all the members prisoners and proclaim Dr. Rintelen Chancellor, he having arrived in Vienna in the meantime. Through one of their spies the Nazis learnt that the meeting of the 24th was postponed until the following day at eleven o'clock in the morning. About 150 assembled in one of the Turner halls in Vienna and after having disguised themselves in uniforms of the Austrian army and police, were loaded on trucks. Thus the troop could easily gain access to the Chancellory.

The government, however, learned about this coup shortly before. Dr. Dollfuss dismissed the cabinet meeting but remained in the Chancellory, where orders for a strict watch of all entrances had been issued. This very order enabled the conspirators to carry out their plan. The officers on guard allowed them to enter, believing that they were military and police attachments sent by the authorities to strengthen the defense of the building. This ruse enabled them to take the military guards prisoners.

Eight terrorists with loaded drawn revolvers stormed into the guard room. Two under-lieutenants, commanders of the guards, carried unloaded revolvers and, therefore, could not offer any resistance. Before they could gain a full understanding of the situation, inasmuch as the rebels wore government uniforms, they were made prisoners. The police and other officials were easily overcome, because their offices were far apart in the labyrinth-like building, and in each case, they were met with a well armed force ready to shoot. The rebels also possessed detailed plans of the Chancellory building.

While one group subjugated the officers of the guard, another rushed into the offices of the Chancellor. When the rebels entered the building, Dr. Dollfuss was in his private office. He went to find out what the trouble was and entered the hall of columns in the company of Secretaries Fey and Karwinsky. When Secretary Fey and several other gentlemen attempted to lock this hall, they met the invading Nazis at the door. The clerks in the hall of columns were overpowered, taken prisoners and compelled to sit around a conference table. Just before this invasion, Secretary of State, Karwinsky, wanted to lead Dr. Dollfuss to a floor above, but the door guard, Hedvicek, intended to rush him into the library of the state archives and thence outside. He grabbed the Chancellor by the arm, But Dr. Dollfuss broke away and hurried back to his office, only to meet his death. After the rebels had entered the hall, one of them, Otto Planetta, who later was executed, quickly stepped up to the Chancellor and without saying a word fired two shots with his pistol. Both shots took effect. Dolfuss turned slightly and then fell backwards. Twice he called for help, but no one paid any attention to him. It was a few minutes before one o'clock when Dr. Dollfuss was wounded. He lay unconscious until a quarter of two before any care was given him. But it was too late. The Chancellor asked for a priest or a physician several times, but these requests were disregarded.

About a quarter to four in the afternoon Dr. Dollfuss breathed his last. He had suffered almost three hours. The refusal of the Nazi murders to call in a priest was especially brutal, since the fervent piety of the Chancellor must have been well known to Hitler's henchmen. The fact that medical attention was also denied him is absolute proof that his murder was part of the plan of the rebels.

What happened afterwards is well known. Due to the intrepidity of President Miklas, the members of the cabinet and Dr. Schuschnigg, who immediately assumed temporary charge of the government, the entire coup was defeated throughout Austria. Rintelen is now a life prisoner in a penal institution. The Austrian government will resist any further attempt of the Nazis to incite a revolt.

Hitler is biding his time. Meanwhile enormous sums are being spent to win over persons in industrial or official life to plot and act against the Austrian government. All the terrorist acts described were planned in Germany by a governmental agency. The assassination of Dollfuss and all the bloodshed in Austria are traceable to this source.

chapter 12

Conclusion

The Swastika betokens dreadful misfortune to all mankind. To liberate Germany from its tragic yoke would be to redeem her people and to preserve civilization. The Nazis aim to turn human progress back a thousand years. They represent the era of right is might, an era in which love and pity were unknown. How insignificant are we humans in comparison to the universe and to God, its Creator! We know nothing. We are powerless. In the history of the universe humanity is like a raindrop falling into the ocean. Jesus Christ preached humility. What right have we to become arrogant and to exalt flesh and blood as noble or sacred? In view of our frailties and failings, we should seek humility and to promote human accomplishment that life may be easier for future generations.

We owe to Christianity the fact that the doctrines of love for one's neighbor and compassion have been promulgated throughout the world and have brought men closer to each other. Although certain medieval periods in the history of the Church were painful intervals, it cannot be denied that the men who communicated the teachings of Christ to the peoples at the risk of their lives have rendered outstanding services to culture. Through Moses and Christ humanity was given the consciousness of kinship with God. Thereby hope was planted in their hearts, that they were more than animals whose existence ended with the passing of their mortal hull. God gave us reason. By applying reason and religious behests, we have succeeded in building a world in which it has become possible to heal the sick, sustain the poor and provide for the aged. Reason and feeling have built the structure which we call culture and civilization.

The Nazis would rob us of both. They seek to despoil humanity of reason and to tear every noble sentiment from our hearts. The Nazis seek to destroy reason by annihilating truth. What is reason without truth? What is reason without a clear correct conception of things and their coherence? The Swastika attacks truth and, thereby, reason, raising deception to a state principle.

The Nazis desire to organize society on the basis of dubious race theories. They have established the teaching that there are superior and inferior races. They teach that the Germans are an exalted race and that the Jews must be exterminated because of their inferior physical and mental heritage. No genuine scholar accepts the racial theory of the Nazis. The colored races are not inferior. They differ from the white race only in color. Within the white race the differences between various groups are but slight. The Jewish Frenchman looks more like his Christian countryman than like his German or Polish co-religionist. Conversely many "Aryan" Germans differ more from each other than from their Jewish compatriots. The Jewish Austrian is closer to his Christian neighbor than is the Prussian.

Murderers, thieves, adulterers, usurers, idiots and maniacs are to be found everywhere. Let us also not forget that decent men, geniuses and intellectual leaders are also found everywhere. There are asylums for the insane and penitentaries for the criminals in all countries and among all peoples. The Chinese murderer is much more like a German criminal than like his law-abiding countryman. An idiotic Mongol is closer to a white idiot than to his normal racial brother. What would Goethe have in common with a Nazi murderer? To Spinoza, a Jew, he felt a close affinity. The criminals and the morally degenerate of all races exhibit a bad heritage.

Naturally, there are Jewish individuals with a bad heritage. That the Nazi accusations against the Jewish people as a whole, however, are founded on lies, I have definitely proven. In the first place it would be ridiculous to assert that there is such a thing as a "Jewish heritage" reaching back to Abraham or Jacob. During the five thousand years of their history the Jews have been thoroughly crossed with all peoples over whom they were victorious or who conquered them. Undoubtedly there are Polish Jews with more Aryan blood than the leader of the Third Reich. The Jews have been mixed with the Philistines, the Persians, the Greeks, the Romans as well as the Germans. Since the emancipation of the Jews from the Ghetto, thousands of Jews have married Gentiles. There is no pure Jewish race any more than there is a pure Aryan race.

Aside from the racial question, I have proven that the Jews, as long as they lived in their own country, were a valorous people. Let us recall the wars of Saul and David and the heroic deeds of the Maccabees. During the World War the Jews fought valiantly on all fronts. They do not take a back seat in the world of sport. The Jewish boxer, Max Baer, recently defeated the German champion, Max Schmeling. That the Jews of the Middle Ages did not exhibit great bodily prowess was not due to any inferiority of heritage. We prevented the Jews from physical development for centuries. We compelled them to live in a dark Ghetto; we excluded them from agriculture, from the crafts and from every honest and wholesome trade.

What about the spiritual heritage of the Jews? They are the creators of the Bible. We, Catholics, see in the Bible a revelation of God. Can we assume that God would have chosen a most unworthy people to transmit his revelations to us? Even those who believe the Bible to be the work of men must all the more admire its creators. In addition to the Bible, the Jews have compiled the Talmud and many other religious guide books, the high ethical value of which cannot be controverted. At the risk of boring my readers, I have quoted a large number of teachings contained in these writings. They testify to an admirable depth of feeling for others, to a purity of character, to an integrity of sentiment and to a rectitude in trade and conduct.

During the Middle Ages the Jews exhibited courage unequalled anywhere. Fearlessly they mounted to the stake, unwilling to forswear their faith. Mothers killed their children and themselves when confronting forcible conversion. The streams of blood that flowed during the Crusades bear adequate proof that the Jewish heritage is by no means inferior. What the Jews have accomplished since their emancipation contradicts every Nazi assertion. Jewish family life is very beautiful. There are few Jewish drunkards or wantons. The Jews have a keen sense of philanthropy and duty to society. They have advanced humanity in the intellectual field. They have given the world great scientists, artists and inventors. They are distinctly law-abiding. Statistics prove that proportionately there are fewer Jewish than Aryan law-breakers. In the face of all this, the thesis of Jewish racial inferiority, a fundamental principle of National Socialism, must be regarded as a vicious lie. A people whose state is based on mendacity can never be happy. Where reason is eliminated, mankind steers toward the abyss. If Nazi-ism were spread over the world, it would be transformed into a madhouse.

The Hitlerites not only rob us of reason but also despoil human sentiment. Can a German child, the silent witness of his Jewish playmate's unjust torture and humiliation, become a good person? Can a National Socialist, who beats, torments or even murders his neighbor in a concentration camp, feel any vestige of love or compassion? Will not his soul be deadened by the constant atrocities, by hatred, barbarity and lust for killing? Mankind requires for its progress not only reason but also love. That which applies to individuals within the nation, also applies to the conduct of nations. Without reason and love of neighbor, there is no effective weapon against war.

National Socialism knows no sentiment and no reason — only hatred, fury and extermination. Consider only the means which the Nazis used to induce Austria to join Germany, and we soon realise how far removed from love and pity they are. Dangerous explosives, hand grenades and infernal machines were sent into Austria with the knowledge that innocent people would be their victims. The cowardly assassination of Chancellor Dollfuss is evidence of Nazi method.

As it is, Christianity pioneered for Hitler when it condoned anti-Semitism. In fact, we nurtured it by hanging a religious cloak about it. We preached love of neighbor, but in our hearts we fostered envy and hatred against a group of humans who committed no wrong. We allowed the serums of Jewish physicians to cure our ills, we accepted everything created by Jewish intellect. At the same time we did every thing to fan hatred of the Jews. This truth must be acknowledged if the evil is to be checked in time. It is not yet too late. So far, we, Austrians, have erected a dam against further encroachment of the Nazis. It is undoubtedly true that the Nazis have succeeded in throwing firebrands among the peoples of all countries. It cannot be denied that the German "agents provocateurs" have been able to carry on propaganda with considerable success.

Three facts have assisted them. First: they have received vast amounts of money from the Third Reich enabling them to spread propaganda on a wide scale. Second: there are the anti-Semitic catch phrases, that have not lost their effectiveness and are thus utilized to excite the masses and arouse passionate fanaticism. Finally: the most important fact is that dreadful poverty makes people receptive to vilifications. These the wily Nazis know only too well how to circulate. If we want to protect ourselves and our children from the atrocities inherent in Nazi-ism, we must do everything possible to obviate hatred of the Jews. Our children must be inoculated with the idea — even before school age — that people are equal before God, and that one must fight only evil individuals. If our children come in contact with Jewish children or adults, we must impress upon them the respect due the Jewish religion and the value of Jews as human beings. A mother permitting the poison of hatred to penetrate her child's heart, must realise that she herself prepares the first nail for her child's coffin. Think of the thousands of young men who during the last few years have perished in Germany on one side or the other! Think of the men working in munitions factories all over the world fashioning instruments of destruction and extermination for millions. If, today, war is palpably near, we owe that danger mainly to the Nazis who are armed to the teeth for the next blood bath.

In the elementary schools the teachers and the priests should protect the children from falling victims to anti-Semitism. In the higher institutions and the universities the Jewish question should be clarified. The provincial clergy has a splendid opportunity to enlighten the peasants. If anti-Semitism were extirpated from all divisions of the populace, the most important weapon of the Nazis would be rendered ineffectual.

The League of Nations should take great pains to wipe out anti-Semitism by drastic legislation. Without anti-Semitism there would be no Hitler today. The alleged advantages which certain sections of the populace would enjoy from the disfranchisement of the Jews are in no way proportionate to the frightful consequences which a victory of the Nazis would entail. The nations should make super-human sacrifices to provide future security rather than to use hatred of Jews as a safety valve for the troubles brought about by the depression.

Take the case of Russia. Why did the Czarist regime fall? Because for decades the Russian people were poisoned by anti-Semitism and vented their spleen in bloody pogroms. This constant incitement made them ripe for the greatest revolution in history. All the Grand Dukes, generals, landowners and industrialists who encouraged the violence of anti-Semitism have paid dearly for their deviltry. They ought to realise today what madness it is to nourish hatred. For the object of this dreadful emotion can easily be changed. If the masses are incited against the Jews over a period of years, the slightest cause may turn their rage upon those who incited them in the first instance. Had the dissatisfactions of the population in Russia been recognized in time and the necessary reforms made, instead of using the Jews as scapegoats, a destructive revolution might not have ensued.

We need not cite Russia. Germany is the best example of the destructiveness of anti-Semitic persecution. For years no one paid any attention to the anti-Semitic agitation of Hitler. To the contrary, efforts were made to emphasize the faults of the Jewish citizens and to ignore completely their excellent qualities. Why did not Germany do in the early days of Hitler what Switzerland, to the joy of the whole civilized world, has done? Without the Protocols of the Elders of Zion, the Nazis could never have risen to power. Educated men in Germany knew that these Protocols were filthy forgeries. Still they stood silent allowing lies about "Jewish World Domination" to be generally disseminated, and the impoverished youth of Germany eagerly believed these fables. The German government permitted the Nazis to spread defamation of the Talmud and pictures of the Jews as monsters and criminals. Had it taken energetic measures to suppress these pests as Switzerland has done, it would not be ruled by them today. Such measures would have guaranteed the permanence of democratic principles.

The gentlemen of the Centrist Party and of the German People's Party, yes, even the gentlemen of the Social Democratic and the German National Party today pay the penalty for their indifference.

Had they wrested the weapon of anti-Semitism from the Nazis in time, the millions of votes that smoothed Hitler's road to power would never have been won. The leaders of the old parties still suffer for the sins of the past. In the last analysis the German people are enduring severe penalties, because the politicians did not realize early enough the dangers of anti-Semitism.

Will the rest of the world benefit by Germany 's experience? I have a feeling that people everywhere are not yet aware of the danger of National Socialism. Instead attempts are made to meet the National Socialist mentality halfway. Such catch-phrases as that the Jews dominated the professions, the press industry, the theatre and commerce in Germany ale popularized abroad.

It is regrettable that these phrases have not been curbed. Jewish leaders themselves admit that the vocational divisions within Jewry are disproportionate. The Jews realize that they do not have large classes of farmers and laborers. The fault of this unwholesome social phenomenon, however, must be laid'to us, the Christians. Until the 12th Century many Jews were farmers, laborers and artisans. During the Middle Ages We forced the Jews into usury and money changing. Only a century ago we liberated them from the Ghetto. No one then thought of arranging the occupational life of the Jews in accordance with any plan. Few Jewish settlements were created, and thus the Jews as a group devoted themselves to trade and to the professions. Lack of foresight and leadership and our still existant prejudice prevented proportionate vocational distribution of Jewry. These conditions are not unalterable. Instead of rebuking the Jews, we should enable their poverty-stricken members to settle in lands where there is still room for colonization.

The British government would render a tremendous service to the Jews and mankind, did they allow the suffering Jewish masses of Eastern and Western Europe to enter Palestine unrestrictedly. There are said to be 1,100,000 people in Palestine. At least four million could be settled there if the territory of Transjordania were to be utilized. Adequate guarantees could be made to the Arab population. Jewish immigration to Palestine has brought nothing but advantages to the Arabs. The value of then-land has increased tremendously, and they have found bread and labor in the upbuilding of Palestine. With millions of immigrants much capital would come, and in a few years a splendid modern state would emerge at the door of Asia in which Jews and \rabs would live peacefully together. England has the most to lose from Nazi expansion. By aiding the Jewish masses of Europe in this way, England could obviate the spread of anti-emitism in Austria, Poland and Roumania and would thus indirectly prevent the territorial encroachment of National Socialism.

Aside from Palestine, the governments of countries threatened by the Nazis should pay special attention to anti-Semitism. The Jews themselves would welcome vocational shifting, providing that their political rights are not invalidated. Such a plan should be carried out gradually. Of course, these matters have been exaggerated. Had Hitler not come to power and had the economic crisis not become so acute, the unnatural vocational distribution of the Jews would scarcely have been noticed. To be perfectly honest I would say that this division of occupations harms only the Jews themselves. The non-Jewish populace is not harmed, for so far we have not found that Jewish physicians treat their patients less skillfully or that Jewish attorneys represent their clients less efficiently than their Christian colleagues. The same is true of Jewish merchants and industrialists. Likewise the legend of the corrupt Jewish press was only dished up to give some unemployed Gentile journalists positions occupied by Jews. In Germany the principle of ousting Jews to make room for unemployed Gentiles was executed in the most brutal manner. Is the German nation any better off now that there are more "Aryan" physicians and lawyers? I doubt it.

The very fact that in critical days Jewish physicians and attorneys are the first targets for persecution should be an incentive to the Jews for a wholesome occupational shift. We, Christians, must be of special assistance to them in this matter. These changes must take place without coercion and without infringment of their political right. They can be accomplished without hatred, without persecution, without the Protocols of Zion, without lies about the Talmud and without the assertion that the Jewish heritage is "inferior."

The world should not be deprived of the benefits of the Jewish mind. The centuries that the Jews spent in the Ghetto led to an imposing development of their intellectual talents. To say that all Jews are clever is a myth. The facts I have cited in this book reveal, however, that in proportion to their numbers, the Jews have a high percentage of intellectual giants.

Despite the fine development of the Jewish intellect, all Jews cannot be physicians, lawyers, editors and scientists. The Jewish masses must be enabled to earn a living by tilling the soil or by working in the factories. We must create conditions, which will give to the Jew, as to others, the possibility of choosing the occupation for which he is best fitted. If the Jew cannot become a peasant, he will have to buy old clothes. If he cannot get into the factories, he will have to join the army of floaters and unemployed. II a Jew cannot learn a decent trade, he will become a peddler. Many people who wanted to go into agriculture or the crafts, make sacrifices to study medicine or law, though they may not be fitted for either profession. Jewish parents strive with tremendous self-sacrifice to send their children to the universities, because they see no other possibility of providing economic security. Gentiles also cannot provide economic security lor their children. The Christian masses also find no employment in factories and offices. Many young Christians attend high school, because they have nothing else to do. The poverty they suffered and the hunger they felt were the best allies that the Nazis had.

There is no doubt that the world is sick. When we burn wheat, destroy cotton, throw coffee into the ocean plow under and shut down factories while millions of men, women and children are starving, it seems that something is wrong with the mechanism of world economy and that this something should be discovered and removed. I have always believed in private enterprise. I am of the opinion that without personal initiative and without the prospect of reward for thrift and efficiency, the progress of the world would be impeded. Yet, I believe that the interests of the industrialists must harmonize with the interests of the workers and the consumers. After much thought on the subject, I have come to the conclusion that the problem of a just and sensible distribution of the world's goods definitely can be solved by tolerance and understanding. We must provide a future for our youth and security for our aged.

National Socialism is the greatest menace of the century. In fighting it, we must use weapons which the Nazis scorn: Idealism and Courage, Common Sense and Love, Truth and Justice!